MW00898798

WOMEN IN THE WEB3 SPACE:
INCLUSIVE FUTURES

AUTHORS

Carley Beck
Débora Betsabé Mercedes Carrizo
Marisa "Ritzy P" Estrada Rivera
Leslie Motta
Sandra Martinez
Wildy Martinez
Ana Isabel Rivas Fernández

Copyright Turkey Hill Press ©2024 All rights reserved.

All rights reserved. No part of this book may be reproduced in any form by electronic or mechanical means, including information storage and retrieval systems, without permission in writing from the publisher, except by a reviewer who may quote brief passages in a review.

DEDICATION

To all the women in the world, always dreaming big. May you find the courage to chase your dreams, the strength to break every barrier, and the wisdom to bloom wherever you are planted. Never give up, nunca se rindan. Your dreams are powerful — let them lead the way.

- Sandra Martinez

CONTENTS

WHO WE ARE

Women of Web3 (WW3) is dedicated to fostering gender equality in the Web3 and Digital Assets sectors.

Founded in April 2023, by Sandra (Sandy) Martinez to participate in the United Nations 78th Science Summit, our mission is to **empower female leaders, creators, and developers by addressing and reducing gender inequalities.**

Aligned with Sustainable Development Goals (SDGs 5 and 10), **we aim to create a diverse, inclusive environment where women and young girls globally can thrive and shape the future of technology.**

ACKNOWLEDGMENTS

This book is a true labor of love, brought to life through the dedication of our founder, Sandy Martinez, and the extraordinary efforts of Marisa Estrada Rivera, with a stunning cover designed by Sandra Barreiro and priceless support from Débora Carrizo and Cyndi Coon. We are deeply grateful to our authors and contributors for sharing their time, thoughts, and stories. We are also grateful for you, our dear reader as with every purchase this book helps fund scholarships for young girls in STEM and uplifts the incredible women who contributed their stories. Thank you all for helping Women of Web3 create magic and impact around the world!

FOREWORD

Sandy Carter, COO of Unstoppable Domains and Founder of Unstoppable Women of Web3 and AI

As I sit down to pen this foreword for "Women of Web3," I'm filled with a sense of excitement and purpose. This book you hold in your hands is not just a collection of stories; it's a mechanism of change, a testament to the power of diversity, and a roadmap for a more inclusive digital future.

My journey in the world of Web3 has been both exhilarating and challenging. As a COO at a leading Web3 company, I've had the privilege of witnessing firsthand the transformative potential of blockchain technology, onchain systems, and the entire Web3 ecosystem. From the early days of cryptocurrencies to the current explosion of Gaming, DeFi, and Digital Identity, I've seen how this technology can democratize access to financial services, revolutionize creative industries, and reshape the very fabric of the internet.

But along this journey, I've also observed a troubling trend: the persistent gender gap in the Web3 space. Despite the promise of inclusiveness and equal opportunity, women remain significantly underrepresented in this burgeoning field. According to a report by Coinbase, women make up only about 15% of Bitcoin traders globally. In the broader tech industry, women hold just 26.7% of tech-related jobs, a percentage that has remained stagnant for years.

This disparity isn't just a matter of numbers; it's a missed opportunity on a massive scale. Research consistently shows that diverse teams outperform homogeneous ones. A study by McKinsey & Company found that companies in the top quartile for gender diversity on executive teams were 25% more likely to have above-average profitability than companies in the fourth quartile.

In the fast-paced, innovation-driven world of Web3, can we afford to leave so much talent and perspective on the sidelines?

The importance of gender equality in the digital landscape, particularly in Web3, cannot be overstated.

Here's why:

1. **Innovation Thrives on Diversity:** Different perspectives lead to more creative solutions and innovative products. In a field as new and rapidly evolving as Web3, we need all the diverse thinking we can get to solve complex problems and create truly revolutionary applications.
2. **Representation Matters:** As Web3 technologies increasingly shape our digital (and physical) world, it's crucial that the builders of these systems reflect the diversity of their users. Without adequate female representation, we risk creating a digital future that doesn't fully account for or serve the needs of half the population.
3. **Economic Empowerment:** Web3 technologies have the potential to democratize access to financial services and create new economic opportunities. Ensuring women are equal participants in this new economy is crucial for global economic equity.
4. **Ethical Considerations:** As we grapple with the ethical implications of AI, data privacy, and decentralized governance, diverse voices are essential to ensure we're creating a digital future that's fair and beneficial for all.
5. **Addressing Existing Inequalities:** Web3 offers a unique opportunity to address and correct existing gender inequalities in tech and finance. By prioritizing inclusivity from the start, we can avoid replicating or exacerbating these disparities in the new digital paradigm.

The stories and insights shared in this book are more than just inspiring tales of individual success. They are a call to action, a reminder that the future of Web3 is not predetermined – it's what we make of it. Each woman featured in these pages has faced challenges, overcome obstacles, and made significant contributions to the Web3 space. Their experiences offer valuable lessons and roadmaps for others looking to enter and thrive in this field.

But beyond individual stories, this book highlights the systemic changes needed to achieve true gender equality in Web3. We need to address the pipeline problem by encouraging more girls and young women to pursue STEM education. According to UNESCO, only 35% of STEM students in higher education globally are women. We must create more inclusive work environments, offer mentorship opportunities, and actively combat biases in hiring and promotion.

Initiatives like Unstoppable Women of Web3 and AI, dedicated to increasing diversity and breaking down barriers to entry in the blockchain and AI space, are leading the way. Their mentorship programs, educational resources, and community events are helping to bridge the gender gap in Web3.

Another initiative is Women of Web3. This is a pioneering initiative that empowers women in the Web3 space through collaboration, education, and advocacy, creating pathways for increased representation and leadership in the digital frontier. By fostering partnerships, opening job opportunities, and aligning with UN Sustainable Development Goals, Women of Web3 is not just shaping the future of technology but also driving societal change.

The stakes are high. Web3 is not just another technological innovation; it's a fundamental reimagining of how we interact, transact, and organize in the digital age. As Sheila Warren, Head of Blockchain and Data Policy at the World Economic Forum, aptly put it, "Blockchain has the potential to reconfigure all human activity as pervasively as did the internet." In this reconfiguration, we have a unique opportunity – and responsibility – to ensure that women are equal architects and beneficiaries of this new digital world.

As you read through the pages of "Women of Web3," I encourage you to see beyond the individual success stories. See the potential for a truly inclusive digital future. See the opportunity to be part of this transformative movement. Whether you're a seasoned Web3 professional, a curious newcomer, or somewhere in between, there's a role for you to play in shaping this space.

- **To the women already making waves in Web3:** your work is invaluable. Continue to innovate, lead, and inspire. Your contributions are not just advancing technology; they're paving the way for countless others to follow.
- **To those considering entering the Web3 space:** take the leap. Your perspective is needed. Your voice is important. The challenges may be significant, but so are the opportunities to make a real impact.
- **To the men in Web3:** be allies. Actively support and amplify women's voices. Recognize and challenge biases, both your own and those you observe in the industry.
- **To everyone:** let's commit to making Web3 a space of true equality and opportunity for all. Let's harness the revolutionary

potential of this technology to create not just a decentralized web, but a more equitable world.

As we stand on the cusp of this new digital frontier, the words of Ruth Bader Ginsburg resonate deeply: "Women belong in all places where decisions are being made." In the world of Web3, where we're making decisions that will shape the future of the internet and beyond, women don't just belong – they're essential.

"Women of Web3" is more than a book; it's a movement. It's a testament to what's possible when we embrace diversity and inclusion in technology. As you turn these pages, I hope you'll be inspired, challenged, and motivated to play your part in creating a Web3 landscape that truly works for everyone.

The future of Web3 is being written right now. Let's ensure it's authored by a diverse and inclusive group of voices. The digital revolution is here, and it needs you – all of you.

CHAPTER ONE

If Not You, Who?
By Carley Beck

To the young woman discovering her power in a world that often seeks to diminish it: may your journey of self-ownership and autonomy flourish in the digital age of blockchain and beyond.

I'm Carley Beck, also known as SuperModelGamer, the Founder of Science | Media | Gaming (SMG.xyz). My journey from a high fashion and runway model in NYC to a Web3 expert and brands strategist at the intersections of tech, fashion, gaming and blockchain has been nothing short of a whirlwind adventure. As a passionate, lifelong gamer and Twitch Affiliate, I've found myself at the forefront of a digital revolution, bridging worlds that once seemed worlds apart.

I've had the honor of speaking at groundbreaking events like the United Nations General Assembly 78th Science Summit, discussing the crucial topics of IP rights, digital assets, blockchain, and fashion. This experience was particularly poignant, as I had once visited the

United Nations as a runway model. Now, I found myself back as a speaker, part of history in the making, sharing insights alongside brilliant minds. The emotional weight of this full-circle moment still resonates with me.

Carley stars in Swedish House Mafia's 'Antidote' vs. Knife Party, ©
2011 Swedish House Mafia.

At the Chopra Foundation - The Future of Wellbeing event, I shared insights on gaming and well-being, exploring how advances in technology and entertainment can enhance our mental and physical health. Deepak Chopra has always been a profound influence on me as a yogi. During the pandemic, my sister and I participated in his 21-day meditation and journaling challenge, which deeply touched us. We were so moved by this bonding experience, my sister made us matching rings inscribed with "This too shall pass" in Sanskrit, reminding us of that time in our lives together, the power of presence, and the resilience to navigate future challenges and triumphs.

Left: Carley photographed by Ariel Garcia. Right: Carley walking for Sarah Jassir Couture
Fall/Winter 2012, © NYTimes

This journey in the Web3 space has been full of learning, with many ups and downs. I've explored various markets and industries with a creative and curious mindset. I'm passionate about owning our stories and identities, both online and offline. That's why I care deeply about issues like IP ownership and tech literacy. I want to make sure our voices and creations stay ours, even as technology advances rapidly with AI and digital innovation.

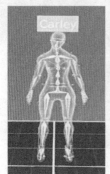

Carley wearing a motion capture (mocap) suit equipped with reflective markers. These sensors track body movements in real-time, allowing for the creation of a digital twin used in digital fashion projects. This technology captures precise movements, enabling designers like Yimeng Yu to dress a virtual model with stunning 0.3mm accuracy.

One of the coolest projects I've worked on, where I successfully negotiated my IP rights, was with Vogue veteran and world-renowned artist Yimeng Yu and digital human studio Modern Mirror. This project allowed me to model for a digital fashion masterpiece, merging traditional aesthetics with cutting-edge technology. Using motion capture and photogrammetry, I was digitized to create a digital twin, allowing Yimeng to dress my virtual self in her stunning digital designs. This experience was both surreal and exciting, blending traditional aesthetics with cutting-edge technology.

Teaming up with Jarritos, Degen Arcade, and Kith at Art Basel, Miami and meeting with the incredible Sandy Martinez for the first time was an inspiring experience. We helped sign guests into the experience via Tokenproof, while learning about each other's varied interests and work in Web3 and traditional Web2. We clicked right away, and we still joke about how random it was to meet this way. Sandy and I would never have any other reason to cross paths, but our shared passion for community and an "in the trenches" style of hands-on learning led us to be fast friends as women in Web3. About half a year later, she offered me the chance to share my story at the UNGA 78th Science Summit.

Carley standing sixth from the left with the inspiring Women of Web3 at the United Nations General Assembly 78th Science Summit in NYC. This summit, held in New York from September 12 to 29, 2023, brought together global leaders to discuss the role of science in achieving the UN's Sustainable Development Goals (SDGs). Carley's panel focused on the transformative potential of blockchain, digital assets, and fashion in the Web3 space, emphasizing collaboration and innovation for a sustainable future.

These Web3 collaborations have shown me the powerful impact of the intersection of digital assets, gaming, blockchain, and AI for those bold enough to dive in. It hasn't been easy, but it has been immensely rewarding and transformative for my career and personal relationships.

This book is a peek into my life—my past experiences, the projects I'm diving into now, and my big dreams for the future of Web3. My hope is that by sharing my advice and story, I can inspire other women and young girls to step into this exciting world and make their mark. We have the potential to create some of the most impactful tools for positive social change, and I can't wait to see what we can achieve together.

Origin Story

I grew up in Surrey, BC, a chaotic suburb around Vancouver known for gang violence and carjacking. My family was barely working class, and my parents were very young when they had my sister and me. However, their love for sports, the outdoors, music, culture, food, and gaming played a crucial role in shaping who I am today. It takes a village to raise a child, especially when your parents are struggling kids themselves, and I credit my upbringing for showing me that community is everything. My parents' youthful spirit (or blind will to survive and adapt) and their excitement for the influences of the 70s, 80s, and 90s around film, music, television, and games were passed on to my sister and me.

From a young age, I was curious and adventurous; a self-proclaimed tomboy and proud of it. My parents were often preoccupied with relationship drama or financial worries, but my grandmothers, Carine Stewart, Edith Beck, and Rena Mason, and my Montessori teacher, Kris Hans, always encouraged me to explore and learn from everything around us. We were taught to learn through books, the arts, technology, and group activities, not just to do as we were told.

I remember spending countless hours reading books like Anne of Green Gables and The Hobbit, watching cartoons like The Magic School Bus and X-Men, visiting Science World to see cool live experiments, and watching science and space movies at the Planetarium. We learned about the importance of nature at the Vancouver Aquarium and were encouraged to use these new things called Personal Computers (PCs) at school and the library. I didn't think about it or know it at the time, but I was already a girl in STEM.

Left: Carley in black and white polka dots at a Montessori school event. Right: Carley with her sister Ashley Beck camping in Northern British Columbia.

I used to take the money I earned from my paper route and chores to buy old three-channel, black-and-white TV sets at garage sales. Taking them apart and playing NES and eventually SNES Nintendo games in my bedroom was a huge treat before cell phones and owning a PC were common. Back then, having your own TV as a kid was a rare luxury. Trading or borrowing games from friends and neighbors was the norm because most families could only afford one or two games at a time. On your birthday, you could rent whatever game you wanted at the local video store, before Blockbuster was even a thing. To give younger generations even more context for how different times were, having a birthday party at McDonald's was the pinnacle of cool and felt luxurious. It's astonishing to think about how oversaturated with media and access we are now compared to those pre-internet days.

I was very much the son my father never had, playing every sport imaginable, staying outside until the streetlights came on, and embracing my inner nerd. I loved understanding how things worked, so I chose high school electives like advanced literature, art, band, drama, metal works, and graphic design while excelling in basketball, volleyball, swimming, and running. My passion for gaming and PCs stood out, despite my varied interests and groups, many of which didn't intersect at the time. People around me often didn't understand my eclectic pursuits, and this judgment persisted until I found the Web3 community.

One of my most vivid memories is when my father brought home the SNES game, "The Legend of Zelda: A Link to the Past." This RPG was an adventurous masterpiece that ignited my passion for games on a whole new level. I was captivated by the virtual worlds, the hero's journey, and the way games could completely capture my imagination, much like great books or the magic of seeing cornstarch turn into an indestructible slime with water for the first time.

I also remember cutting out models and fashion campaigns from magazines, collaging them into beautiful new creations, categorizing them from fitness to beauty, and building my own magazine publications. I aspired to be an Editor in Chief like Graydon Carter or Anna Wintour, blending my love for creativity and storytelling into every project.

Carley at Hideo Kojima's Death Stranding World Tour NYC with Ludens 2019.

I regularly skipped school to play games, sneaking back into the house after pretending to leave for school (everyone had to walk to school back then). I'd climb through a small window of our house to quickly hide inside a closet or kitchen cupboards, waiting for them to leave for work. I already knew I could never get enough of gaming, no matter how many times I got caught or yelled at, and it turns out I was right!

It was during these formative years I realized the power of technology and innovation to transform lives and create new opportunities, particularly my own. Growing up with parents always screaming at one another, being around negative influences like violence, drugs and alcohol, and the pervasive financial insecurity of "kids" raising two kids made imagination and escapism the most important skill to develop if I were to avoid the same fate or worse. The funny thing about growing up this way is how normalized the extremes around you are, and I vividly remember countless fights with my parents ending with "at least I'm not pregnant!"

It wasn't until I was able to process so much of my early upbringing and young adult life as an adult that I realized how lucky I am to have found these early influences to expand my consciousness, develop cognitive and social skills, and constantly redefine what values and world I lived in through the books and games I consumed. Had I not felt a strong sense of self through my interests and communities, I know I would not have made it out of the limited environment and dangerous situations I saw many of my friends and family in.

Challenges from childhood shaped me in positive ways, whether I knew it at the time or not, but through creativity, my mind found solace and stimulation to balance out the chaos. It was this balance that allowed me to persevere, grow, and eventually thrive despite the hardships.

This fact alone is a huge part of why it's so important to me to spread the power of digital identity and self-ownership, and I cringe every time I hear people say gaming is a waste of time or just for kids. Perhaps to those who have access to support, opportunities and safe communities it is hard to understand, but to the millions, if not billions, of those in this world who do not, it is often the only community, positive reinforcement, and safe space we have.

Embrace the challenges you face, as they can be powerful catalysts for growth. Creativity can be a sanctuary, providing balance and clarity during turbulent times. Use your passions and interests as tools to navigate difficulties and remember that perseverance through adversity often leads to profound personal growth and strength. Find your creative outlets and let them guide you towards resilience and self-discovery.

The Creative Leap – Education and Early Career

I pursued my education at Fordham University, focusing on English Literature. Fordham provided a strong foundation in critical thinking, analysis, and storytelling. These skills later proved invaluable in my career. My time at Fordham was filled with opportunities to explore the depths of literature and its impact on culture and society.

However, the global financial crisis hit during my time at Fordham, leading me to pivot from my dream of attending Fordham Law back into modeling—a field I had dabbled in as a teenager in Vancouver. Small jobs for MAC cosmetics and local runway shows were the most exciting part of my teenage life, outside of sports and gaming, but I was often told it wasn't a "real" career and not to let it get to my head. Ironically, it was modeling and fashion that became my purpose and guiding light when all else failed. Deep down, it was the thing I wanted to pursue the most.

Growing up, I was mesmerized by Fashion TV, idolizing models like Frankie Ryder and Naomi Campbell, designers such as Marc Jacobs, Armani, and John Galliano, and photographers like Helmut Newton, Steven Meisel, and David LaChapelle. These creative icons were my inspiration. When I felt uncertain, I relied on my creativity and passion for storytelling through art and fashion. I dedicated myself entirely to becoming a high fashion and runway model, ignoring those who doubted my potential, my looks, or my strength.

Embrace your passions, even if they seem unconventional. Often, it's the things we love most that guide us when we're lost. Trust your instincts, and don't be afraid to pursue what truly excites you.

Carley jumping from a Cessna in her pink NBCF skydiving suit during USPA license training at Skydive Crosskeys, New Jersey. Right: From interview and editorial with Work Week Chic.

Being a working model meant constantly pushing for better clients and collaborations, seeking more press, and pursuing top-tier teams for shows and shoots. It involved building relationships with everyone from makeup artists to producers, essential for evolving as an artist and booking more work. You're judged on everything—consistency, charisma, endurance, and physique. It never truly gets easy; it just becomes easier to view your work objectively and understand the importance of self-care, especially if you've developed a positive mindset. To succeed, you must become a better instrument of creativity while embodying the ideals of those around you, both on and off the runway. It's as intellectually and emotionally taxing as it is physically demanding and politically nuanced.

The biggest misconception about models is the belief that they must fit a specific, tangible standard. While there are industry guidelines for different markets—commercial, glamor, runway, and high fashion—these standards are more about business segmentation than personal judgment. The fashion industry's overproduction and waste stem more from the public's obsession with mass-produced "high fashion" than from the industry's standards. It's important to recognize that there is now a market for everyone and everything. Forcing every market to cater to everyone is unsustainable and inauthentic, damaging the planet and devaluing skilled workers. In the age of e-commerce, options are plentiful, but when I was a teenager, finding the right fit often meant resorting to men's shoes for sports or shopping at specialty stores for jeans. Times have changed.

Left: Carley walking for Elizabeth Kosich 2012 at NYFW. Middle: Vo Viet Chung 2014 for Couture Fashion Week, Right: Vintage Couture Showcase at Couture Fashion Week 2016.

Typically, the most competitive models fit within a range of height and measurements that allow them to work across multiple markets. However, each market has its distinct look, standards, and key players, creating a diverse and rich landscape where one can find their unique place. Success in modeling, like in many fields, requires showing up consistently, working hard, networking, and believing in yourself for many years. Even as you progress, the pressure to outdo your last job remains, defining your professionalism.

Interview and 6-page photo editorial of Carley Beck in her apartment at the time in East Harlem, featured in Editors Favorites and Homepage of Vice Mexico.

Once you find the markets that you work well in, navigating the expectations of others, yourself, and the practical details of "the job" are what really determine your success. Moreover, I saw the mental and emotional pressure of tunnel vision, and this strange dual existence, destroying many models long before competing looks, aging or changing markets ever affected their careers. My strength over time was in my diversity and willingness to adapt, not to fit one market or one standard but to be a hard worker and flexible with my expectations of what I "should" be.

My experiences in modeling taught me invaluable lessons about perseverance, self-worth, and the power of creativity. Whether on the runway or in a photoshoot, I learned to express myself authentically and embrace the challenges that came my way. These experiences were not just about looking good but about conveying a story, a mood, and a message through art, movement and creativity. By embracing my uniqueness and developing a ton of resilience, I was able to carve out a successful career in an industry that initially seemed daunting, unwelcoming, and unforgiving.

Understand that success doesn't come from fitting a single mold. Each industry has its unique standards and finding your niche both in and around the norms can be incredibly empowering. Don't be afraid to explore different avenues and discover where you shine.

Before we get to my paradigm shift from Web2 to Web3, I want to make sure I continue to set the stage. I was already over a decade and a half into my career as a model before I had ever heard the words "decentralized web" or "blockchain."

Like most working models, I still had to subsidize my income while modeling. I took on various roles in writing, copy editing for magazines, web writing, and production coordination. Through my writing, I worked with Patti Smith and Steven Sebring, maintained a gaming blog covering games like Destiny, Call of Duty, Paragon, and Overwatch, and helped copyedit indie fashion magazines like *Suited*.

Left: Carley walking for Benitos Santos 2018. NYFW Middle: Marisol Henriques 2016, Couture Fashion Week. Right: Arega Couture 2020, FLDA.

Through production coordination, I worked with Cindy Crawford, Alicia Keys, and Whitney Houston. I managed the call sheets, logistics, and worked insanely long hours. These roles not only provided financial stability but also gave me invaluable insights into the industry. I learned to navigate the intricacies of storytelling, editing, and managing creative projects. Each creative project I took on broadened the scope and scale of my modeling career. By reverse engineering aspects of the creative process from other creatives, I could bring their insight into my own career, ultimately making me a better model and creative.

In addition to my creative professional work, I've volunteered for over ten years for various outreach organizations using my time, platform, and money to help others. This includes work with Bloomingdales Runway Warriors, A Free Bird Pediatric Cancer Charity, mentoring and volunteering for kids with cancer interested in the arts, NBCF, Games to Grunts, and 76 Operators.

Working with various organizations has profoundly reshaped my perspective on what I could achieve beyond my career and financial stability. I recognized many opportunities to help others simply by showing up, offering insights, and allowing others to glimpse into my world. I walked the runway with kids who had barely left the hospital, watched children ring "the bell" to proudly announce they had beaten cancer, and reunited with a young girl who had once helped with my makeup while she still had a port-a-cath in her chest—only to see her beat cancer, grow up, and open her own bakery.

These experiences in outreach have been some of the most fulfilling of my life, making me happier and more grateful. I wonder why more people don't integrate this kind of work into their lives, and how much more joyful and present they could be if they did.

Left: Bloomingdale's Runway Warriors with Kate Spade and Ralph Lauren supporting kids with Cancer. Right: Modeling Sarah Jassir with kids from A Free Bird Pediatric Cancer Org.

However, despite these rewarding experiences, I often faced public rejection and judgment as a model. You require a tough skin to believe in yourself, no matter what you are doing, and one of my favorite things to say is, "Life is what happens when you're making other plans." The older I get, the truer this expression becomes. I was ridiculed and looked down on for "needing" to work outside of modeling—just as I was criticized for enjoying games or reading too many books. Even now, I am often attacked online for my looks, simply for being a model in gaming or Web3. People mistakenly perceive me as leveraging gaming and Web3 to gain traction for my modeling career, rather than recognizing how my decades-long modeling experience adds unique value and insight to these industries.

Simultaneously, I am continually proving myself intellectually to communities that overlook my contributions beyond my appearance. Despite my many achievements, I still face skepticism about my ability to speak intelligently while being a front-facing, commercially saleable, media-trained personality. Countless times, people have asked why I don't want to be an influencer or Key Opinion Leader (KOL) rather than acknowledging my accomplishments as a passionate tech literacy advocate, digital art collector and leader in the space—independent of my modeling career—as justification enough for my presence here.

It's ironic how, in my pursuit to make a broader impact through gaming, blockchain, and digital culture, I find myself defending my intellect and capabilities. Yet, this continuous challenge has only strengthened my resolve. I've learned to embrace the duality of my public persona and my technical expertise, using both to advocate for the integration of innovative technologies in creating positive social change. Some may feel compelled to flaunt their expertise within echo chambers, but I believe true influence comes from tangible contributions, not from proving one's intellectual dominance on X threads or copy/paste panels for press's sake.

From Icon Magazine's, "She Walks in Beauty." The 8-page photo editorial stars Carley as model, creative director, and editor photographed by Meera Fox, makeup by Sandy Nicha.

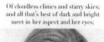

From Icon Magazine's, "She Walks in Beauty." The 8-page photo editorial stars Carley as model, creative director, and editor photographed by Meera Fox, makeup by Sandy Nicha.

From my relentless encounters with projections and stereotypes, I've learned that your skills, personality, network, looks, and experiences are uniquely yours and should be celebrated. It's easy for brands, organizations, and individuals to try to make you feel like you owe them an explanation for who you are and why you belong. However, it's essential to remember that you don't need to justify your existence or your journey to anyone. Embrace your individuality and take pride in the multifaceted person you are.

Reflecting on my career, I experienced extreme highs and lows that I debated whether to delve into deeply in this book. However, sharing the reality of my experiences is crucial. I fought through eating disorders, drug abuse, homelessness, bad relationships, and even violence and sexual trauma. From 2015 to 2021, I spent six years at the Trauma Psychotherapy Military Clinic at NYU Langone for PTSD every week after being attacked and raped by a stranger. The journey to recovery was long and arduous, dealing with both physical and mental challenges. Although I will never fully understand why it happened or receive justice for what I endured, I have found strength and resilience in the aftermath.

Left: Carley practicing yoga. Right: Carley practicing maneuvers in freefall.

During my healing journey, I earned my yoga teacher certification and skydiving license, each representing milestones of self-discovery and resilience. Changing friend groups many times, I sometimes felt isolated, unsure if I could have friends at all. Other times, my friends were the lifeline that kept me from falling apart completely. Every day in those early years of recovery was a choice to evolve or die, teaching me more about myself and others than any other experience. Through sheer determination, I didn't just survive—I healed. I found a deeper, richer appreciation for life and learned to love myself profoundly.

One of the most valuable lessons from my therapy with Dr. Margo Kakoulis and the military clinic team was the importance of setting strong boundaries. Many of us, especially women, often feel compelled to share our most tragic and painful moments to justify our needs, compassion, or drive. Upon graduating from trauma psychotherapy, I promised myself that my story would be one of hope and beauty, focusing on positivity and resilience.

Despite the challenges and adversities, I've faced, I believe in the extraordinary potential within each of us. We can continue to show up for ourselves, even when things are far from perfect. We have the power to redefine ourselves repeatedly, growing larger than the individual circumstances of our accomplishments *and* our most painful traumas.

*Top Left Clockwise: Carley for Victoria Spector Swimwear 2014.
Middle: Beauty Campaign for Make-Up Pro 2019, Bottom: From Dark
Matter Fashion Editorial for Theme Magazine 2021.*

*Your journey is a testament to your strength and resilience.
While your experiences have shaped you, they don't define
you. Embrace the beauty and triumphs of your story, for it is
yours to share on your own terms. When we choose to define
ourselves through our positive actions and words, we
transcend victimhood. Share your story because it empowers
you, not because you seek validation. You are enough.*

The pandemic brought unprecedented challenges and opportunities. The need for social connection and the rise of digital platforms inspired me to start my Twitch channel, SuperModelGamer. I immersed myself in learning Adobe products and OBS (Open Broadcast Software) to produce high-quality content, create animations for my chat, and design my on-screen UI overlays. The initial setup and learning curve were challenging, but the process was incredibly rewarding. Streaming allowed me to blend my passions for gaming, hardware, and editing software while creating a unique space for my online community. I learned through online courses, tinkering with programs and hardware, and asking online friends for help.

Carley's first 3D/AR NFT was published on OpenSea. An art piece inspired by the Adidas/Prada Re-Nylon and Zach Lieberman's community project, created in Adobe Substance.

As I honed my skills with Adobe Suite, I gained confidence in digital art creation and editing software. This newfound confidence led me to explore Adobe Substance, a cutting-edge tool for 3D design. Despite my lack of experience in 3D modeling, I was captivated by its potential, especially its ability to convert designs into augmented reality (AR). To accelerate my learning, I downloaded assets from Creative Commons, allowing me to reverse engineer and understand the intricacies of 3D design.

During this period, I discovered the work of Beeple, also known as Mike Winkelmann. His stunning 3D assets and groundbreaking approach to digital art sparked my passion for blockchain technology. Beeple's "Everydays" auction, which sold for $69 million, was a pivotal moment for me. The fact that his work was associated with blockchain technology intrigued me, and I became determined to understand this revolutionary system.

My curiosity led me to dive deep into the world of blockchain. I followed Beeple's journey, learned about the platforms he used, went to his first physical art show in Tribeca, NY and started taking courses offered by the Web3 Foundation. I immersed myself in the Web3 community, joining discords, attending virtual meetups, and consuming vast amounts of digital content. Podcasts like Bankless,

Overpriced JPEGS, Gen C, Kevin Rose and Real Vision combined with insights from figures like Vitalik Buterin, Beeple, Punk6529, Keith Grossman and Refik Anadol became my guides in this new frontier.

Carley engaged with her online gaming community
SuperModelGamer on Twitch.tv.

Collecting digital art on platforms like Nifty Gateway was exhilarating. For the first time, I could engage with art in a way that aligned with my passions for gaming and digital design. I researched artists, attended NFT drops, and engaged with the community to better understand the landscape. This journey of discovery was both fun and educational, helping me become more discerning and mature in my understanding of the industry.

I went to as many meetups, art shows, conferences and galleries as I could, and I still do. Everything from Veecon, Consensus, Christies Art + Tech, NFTNYC and Art Basel, to Beeple Studios, Sotheby's, Pace, and the Moma. These events covered a range of topics, from music and poetry NFTs to the work of prominent collectors and artists. Engaging with the community in person allowed me to form meaningful relationships and deepen my knowledge of the space.

Top Left: Carley and Mike Winkleman at Beeple's first gallery show at Jack Hanley, Tribeca NY. Top Right: Beeple Studios opening night. Bottom Left: Refik Anadol and Carley at the Moma. Middle: Carley in front of Refik Anadol's Unsupervised - Machine Hallucinations at the Moma. Right: Carley and Keith Grossman at Veecon, Minneapolis 2022.

The early days of Web3 were challenging and full of scams. The user experience (UX) and user interface (UI) were often clunky, bridging between platforms was difficult, and gas fees were high. Despite these hurdles, I persevered, driven by my passion for learning and my belief in the transformative power of blockchain technology. The landscape has evolved significantly since then, but those early experiences taught me the value of patience, curiosity, and active participation in the community.

Entering any new industry requires dedication, passion, and a willingness to be a perpetual student. It's never too late to catch up or make a meaningful impact. By staying active in relevant communities and being open to new ideas, I transitioned from being a follower to a builder in the Web3 space.

Current Ventures

Today, my journey in the Web3 space continues to unfold in exciting and unexpected ways. As the Founder of Science | Media | Gaming (SMG.xyz) and SuperModelGamer, I draw on my diverse background to engage in projects that resonate deeply with my passions and values. Each project I take on is a new chapter in my ongoing story, filled with opportunities for creativity and connection.

Community engagement remains at the heart of my work. Curating nearly a year of digital art from my personal collection at Crypt Gallery Dream Downtown NYC reinforced my love for storytelling. Showcasing the vibrant and diverse world of digital art, and artists, emphasized the importance of digital ownership and the role of blockchain in preserving the integrity of creative works. This allowed me to connect with artists and art lovers alike, fostering a deeper understanding and appreciation of digital art.

Equally rewarding has been my work with TIMEPieces. As a founding Community Council member and TIMEPieces Council Person of the Year 2023, I've had the honor of guiding this initiative's growth. TIMEPieces brings together artists, collectors, and fans in a collaborative spirit. Hosting panels, curating special events, designing community voted discord emotes, and creating the first open to all, IRL TIMEPieces monthly meetups in NYC has been incredibly fulfilling. These gatherings attracted some of the most notable artists and advocates in Web3, fostering a vibrant, supportive community that thrives on creativity and shared passion.

Left: Carley and Vasia Makris, Co-founder of Crypt Gallery and Moments Agency. Right: Warm Crypto panel from Carley's TIMEPieces Takeover event, featuring 11 speakers over 2 days.

A particularly inspiring experience was my collaboration with Beastmode and Marshawn Lynch's Fam 1st Family Foundation at VeeCon. This partnership aimed to empower young Black entrepreneurs by providing them with opportunities to attend VeeCon, leveraging our networks, and meeting influential figures like Gary Vaynerchuk. This project exemplified blockchain technology's potential for driving social impact and community engagement. It underscored the critical role of mentorship and networking, while demonstrating how technology can empower community development and nurture future leaders.

BOUTTHATWEB3 event at VeeCon 2023. Carley, middle back row, with fellow mentors and 50 local, black entrepreneurs. T3mpo, Gary Vee, Marshawn Lynch and featured mentors sponsored and hosted a two-day program connecting web3 "OG's" and young business leaders to attend VeeCon while leveraging the networks of established web3 leaders and crypto artists.

My involvement with the Polkadot's Dot Play team represents another exciting venture. This project is a groundbreaking step in merging blockchain technology with gaming. We are creating engaging and innovative digital experiences that highlight the transformative potential of decentralized systems. I believe gaming is one of our most powerful onboarding tools in Web3, and through UGC (Roblox) and UEFN (Fortnite), we will see the rise of digital assets and independent creators on an unprecedented scope and scale.

In addition to these initiatives, my current advisory roles with Mythical Games, Signum Growth, and the Chopra Foundation allow me to share insights on brand strategy, trend forecasting, and the importance of tech literacy at the intersections of digital culture, blockchain, gaming, and fashion. These positions enable me to influence forward-thinking initiatives that align with the core values of decentralization, accessibility, and transparency.

Top Left: Dot Play members John Linden (Mythical Games CEO), Carley Beck, Angela Dalton (Signum Growth), Conor Daly (Indycar/NASCAR Driver), Aaron Goolsbey (Mythical Games COO). Top Right: Carley reporting on digital fashion trends live on SMG. Bottom Left: Carley speaking at the Chopra Foundation - Future of Wellbeing event in NYC. Bottom Right: Carley with Poonacha Machaiah, CEO of the Chopra Foundation.

Streaming and education remain at the heart of my mission. Through my Twitch.tv channel, SuperModelGamer, and the content I create for SMG.xyz, I explore online culture and diverse industries for a global audience. By sharing my knowledge of gaming, digital art, fashion and blockchain technology, I've cultivated a community of learners and innovators, empowering them to explore these dynamic fields. I've also developed four comprehensive, free courses on NFTs, AI, Cryptocurrency, and the Metaverse, available on my website. Additionally, I contribute weekly articles to ChopraPost.com (the Chopra Foundation) on the positive impact of gaming on mental health and community building, as well as weekly articles to SMG.xyz covering a wide array of tech and digital culture topics.

Looking Ahead – Future Aspirations

Looking ahead, I am filled with excitement and optimism for the future of Web3. The intersection of fashion, gaming, blockchain, and AI holds immense potential for driving positive social change, and I am eager to continue exploring and contributing to this evolving landscape.

The Goddess Cave aka. Carley's home studio and office in NYC, featuring her gaming battle station and favorite gaming books 2022.

The evolution of Web3 is just beginning, and its potential is vast. I envision a more inclusive and accessible digital landscape where technology bridges connections across different backgrounds and geographies. The principles of decentralization, transparency, and global accessibility will continue to drive innovation and create opportunities for everyone.

I envision blockchain technology expanding well beyond financial, social or cultural applications to revolutionize education, healthcare, and environmental sustainability. By leveraging blockchain's immutable and transparent nature, we can build systems that are more equitable, open and resilient, effectively addressing some of the most pressing global challenges.

Wildy Martinez, Carley Beck and Lucia Diaz speaking at the UNGA 78th Science Summit 2023.

As I continue my education in Python and C# with an insatiable curiosity for physics engines and AI, I aim to enhance my ability to contribute to meaningful digital culture and experiences. I'm particularly interested in how gaming, digital culture, and pop culture can serve as gateways to the Web3 space, fostering better systems for mental health care, accelerating scientific discovery, verifying content authenticity, transforming education and bolstering outreach initiatives.

AI's ability to process vast amounts of data can drive insights and efficiency, while blockchain ensures that this data is managed with integrity and transparency. Together, these technologies can revolutionize how we approach problems and develop solutions, fostering a new era of technological and social progress. This integration can lead to better environmental care through more efficient resource management and real-time monitoring. Enhanced security and privacy measures will protect personal data without compromising oversight, and individuals will have greater opportunities to participate in the global economy, fostering more inclusive growth and development.

As we stand on the brink of these technological advancements, what role do you see yourself playing in shaping this future? How can you leverage your unique skills and experiences to contribute to the development of more equitable and sustainable systems?

Conclusion: Embracing the Digital Frontier

Reflecting on my journey, I am grateful for the incredible experiences and opportunities that have shaped my path. From the early days of navigating the fashion industry to diving deep into the world of Web3, each step has been a testament to the power of perseverance, curiosity, and community.

The future of Web3 is bright, and I am excited to be a part of this transformative movement. By continuing to push the boundaries of what is possible and advocating for inclusivity, transparency, and innovation, I hope to inspire others to join this journey and make their mark on the digital landscape.

To the women and aspiring innovators reading this, remember that your voice matters. Embrace your passions, pursue your dreams, and never stop learning. The digital age offers limitless possibilities, and together, we can create a future that is equitable, sustainable, and full of opportunity.

Call To Action

Join me in exploring the boundless potential of Web3, and let's build a world where technology serves as a force for good, empowering individuals and communities to thrive. My goal is to harness the power of gaming, blockchain, and digital culture to create a positive impact at scale. Given gaming's unparalleled engagement, global reach, and appeal to all ages, I believe blockchain-integrated gaming will become a crucial tool for education, outreach, and economic development.

DYOR, GGs and GLHF <3

UNGA SCIENCE SUMMIT 78 SPEECH   September, 2023

When I first entered the web3 space, I was custom-building overlays for my gaming channel, testing out Unreal Engine, and creating digital art for personal development, not considering its impact on my fashion modeling career.

Over the last decade and a half, I've been featured in Vogue, Vice, Elle, Fashion TV, WWD, MTV, and The New York Times for my print and runway work. Yet, I'm also a lifelong gamer, recognized for my creative direction, copywriting, retouching, and production work.

Despite generating nearly $2 billion in revenue last year, the modeling industry remains unregulated, rife with physical, emotional, and financial abuse. Models often face delays or non-payment, lack legal protections, and endure inhumane working conditions, irrespective of professional experience or representation. We rely on the hope that those we work with will treat us fairly, pay us what we're owed, and credit our work properly.

Many top fashion brands, agencies, and media companies perpetuate mistreatment, unfair pay, and poor working conditions, exploiting a high turnover rate of vulnerable, young people. Models have minimal control over our IP rights, lack transparency in payments, and often receive advances on pay that force us into debt. Agencies then charge interest and divert clients that could help models repay these advances, trapping us in a cycle of financial exploitation.

This exploitation parallels the traditional art world, sports industries, and freelance work, all suffering under gatekeepers and third-party systems. During COVID-19, the fashion industry halted, and I discovered blockchain and web3. I saw artists and athletes using blockchain to sell digital art and moments on platforms like Nifty Gateway and Top Shot directly to their audiences, attributing tangible value through ERC-721 tokens.

Blockchain technology was a revelation, offering an open, digital ledger to prove provenance, IP ownership, and real-time financial value, enabling global distribution without intermediaries. I committed to learning how this technology could benefit my work as a fashion model, gamer, and creative, not just for myself, but to educate others and support tech literacy.

I started with open learning courses from the Web3 Foundation, began collecting blockchain art, and learned to create smart contracts. I attended conferences, joined web3 communities, and immersed myself in blockchain. When brands experimented with metaverse platforms and digital fashion in games like Fortnite and Roblox, I sought the best virtual scanning company at Digital Fashion Week in New York to digitize myself and discuss web3's ethical and business benefits. I negotiated ownership and oversight of my digital modeling assets, known as my Digital Human.

Through my web3 journey, I've booked major digital modeling campaigns, built a vast digital asset portfolio, connected with prolific artists and industry leaders, and earned the honor of representing TIME magazine's TIMEpieces Community Council as an art collector in their historic web3 art and outreach division.

I stand here at the UNGA Science Summit, proud to share my experience in the web3 space, representing the merging cultures and industries that can leverage this innovative technology to empower individuals exploited by third-party systems. Culture is a powerful connector, and through it, I aim to champion tech literacy, decentralization, and self-sovereignty. With blockchain, we can all have a place and a voice, ownership and oversight of our data, and most importantly, true value.

SuperModelGamer, Carley Beck   SMG.xyz

Carley's prepared speech for the UNGA Science Summit 78 was timed to exactly 2 minutes. Due to teleprompter issues, it was never used, and the panel format was improvised.

Let's Connect

Carley Beck
www.womenofweb3un.io/speakers/carley-beck
Science|Media|Gaming - @SuperModelGamer - SMG.xyz

CHAPTER TWO

From Passion to Purpose: Humble Beginnings to Leading Innovation in Web3
By Débora Betsabé Mercedes Carrizo

My name is Débora Betsabé Mercedes Carrizo, and I am a proud software engineer, entrepreneur, and leader. My journey has taken me across borders and cultures, providing me with the incredible opportunity to work on international projects for tech industry giants such as IBM and Accenture, as well as banks focusing on developing countries like the Inter-American Development Bank and the African Development Bank.

My story is a testament to how technology can open doors, create pathways, and transform lives, just as it did for me.

This is not about my professional achievements. It's about the resilience, determination, and passion that fueled my journey. It's about the mentors and leaders who believed in me, the challenges that tested my resolve, and the innovations to which I was fortunate enough to contribute.

Most importantly, it's about sharing the message that no matter where you start or when, no matter which country or city you were born in, regardless of your gender or race, technology can be a powerful equalizer. It empowers you to build the future you envision for yourself.

Through these pages, I aim to inspire aspiring technologists, especially those from underrepresented backgrounds. My goal is to demonstrate that anyone can rise to become an expert in the tech industry with dedication, hard work, and discipline. My story serves as a beacon of hope, a call to action, and a roadmap for those who dare to dream beyond their current circumstances.

My story is not just about personal success; it's a tribute to my family's legacy. It's about honoring the sacrifices they made and the lessons they imparted. It's about carrying forward their resilience and determination as I carve out my own path in the tech industry.

Now, I stand here today, reflecting on a career that spans over 25 years in the dynamic and ever-evolving field of technology, a field predominantly dominated by men.

Roots and Wings

I am my parents' first child. I come from a small family; we are Spanish descendants, but my grandparents were born in Argentina, so we are a very Argentinian family coming from different regions in my country.

My grandparents migrated to Mendoza with nothing but hope and determination, instilling in us the values of hard work and education. I remember my grandfather joking about his school days, admitting he was a poor student. Yet, his stories resonated deeply with me. I saw it as my mission to go further, not just beyond his achievements but also beyond my father's, to seize better opportunities. In my mind, our family was a work-in-progress family, each generation building upon the last. Like constructing a staircase, we were committed to advancing from one level to the next, each step representing our collective progress and dedication to a brighter future.

We were a working-class family. Even when we had what they considered essential, and my path to university wasn't restricted by financial barriers, as many degree programs in my country are tuition-free, striving for better opportunities was always my mindset. I constantly asked myself, "Why not? What do I need to know and do? How can I achieve more?" This drive to seek and embrace opportunities fueled my ambition to push our family legacy forward.

On my mother's side, I come from a lineage of strong women. My grandmother and mother exemplified resilience and strength in their unique ways. Being a strong woman isn't only about holding positions of power like a CEO; it's about embodying strength, determination, and grace in everyday life. They served as powerful role models, teaching me that strength comes in many forms and forging me into the strong woman I am today.

My mom was always by my side, nurturing and protecting me while allowing me to explore my interests and be true to myself. She embraced my uniqueness, encouraging me to pursue what I loved most. As a shy and introverted girl who enjoyed studying and playing alone, especially as an only child for seven years, she gave me the space to grow and develop at my own pace. She instilled in me the belief that my individuality was a strength and that I could achieve anything I set my mind to. Her unwavering support and understanding helped me build the confidence to embrace my true self.

My dad, a young, intelligent musician, and an intellectual man took the time to share his knowledge with me. He taught me English, music, math, and some life lessons. He instilled in me the belief that studying was essential for achieving good evaluations and that preparation was crucial for success. From a young age, he emphasized the importance of training and preparation. Whether it was for an exam or a game, he taught me never to step into any challenge without being thoroughly prepared. His guidance planted the seeds of diligence and perseverance in me, shaping my approach to every endeavor I pursued.

And they both gave me the support to make me feel that I was capable of anything I decided to focus on.

Despite the challenges we faced, my family's unwavering support was my anchor. They believed in my dreams, even when the path seemed unclear and starting a career in software in 1994 was a bit unknown. Their faith in me was the fuel that kept me going, pushing me to achieve what seemed complicated.

"The Beginning of a Journey"

In this photo, Debora's parents hold her as a one-year-old, unaware of the path their love and support would guide her. This moment marks the foundation of resilience and possibility that would shape her future in technology and global impact

I remember that when I was a kid, my parents used to buy me a magazine called "Anteojito y Antifaz." This magazine was created as a learning support for kids. Inside, there was a chapter to create your experiment, and every week was a different one. I was so excited to see what the experiment was in each edition.

That made me so proud of myself because I was able to follow the steps and build something on my own. I savored the solitude that delivered the mastering of those experiments while the house stood quiet while my parents were sleeping. That gave me the confidence to think that I could handle any "experiment" by myself in my "own imaginary lab." From those moments to these days, something has not changed. My shelter has always been alone and learning something new; education is my shelter.

When I feel insecure, I study
When I feel sad, I study
When I am afraid of having the capacity to solve something, I study
When I feel challenged by a problem, I study

I always thought that education was my fuel for a better future, so everything around me that I didn't like would be a problem to solve or change in the future.

I attended the neighborhood school, a mere 14 blocks from home, and each day, my mother accompanied me on foot. The journey to school became a cherished routine when we talked about everything from the day ahead to our dreams for the future. Despite the distance, I looked forward to those walks—moments filled with anticipation and connection.

Arriving at school was always a joyous occasion, especially at the start of a new school year. One of my favorite rituals was shopping for school supplies. The local bookstore became a treasure trove of possibility, lined with shelves of neatly organized notebooks, colorful pens, and crisp textbooks waiting to be explored. I remember the thrill of carefully selecting each item.

As I grew older, these yearly trips to the bookstore symbolized more than just preparation for the academic year. They represented a tangible link between my aspirations and the tools needed to achieve them. Each new set of supplies held the promise of learning, discovering, and growing, a promise I eagerly embraced as a young girl, being eager to absorb everything the world had to offer.

Since those years, I have fostered enthusiasm for learning, and my family has played a significant role in nurturing my educational journey. They encouraged my curiosity and celebrated my achievements, providing a solid foundation for my academic pursuits. Being a good student was more than just getting good grades. It was about the confidence that came with knowing I could tackle new challenges and overcome them. Completing assignments and preparing for tests was a process I approached with diligence and enthusiasm, knowing that each success added another brick to the foundation of my self-assurance.

I approached my assignments with diligence and prepared thoroughly for any kind of test. It seemed that learning came naturally to me, and I often found myself excelling in my schoolwork. I felt fortunate to be able to understand and grasp concepts with ease, which made learning more enjoyable.

It wasn't long before I realized that I consistently ranked among the top students in my class. This realization dawned on me one day when, at primary school, I recognized that my efforts had placed me not just at the top of my class but as the best student in the entire school. This was a humbling moment, and I felt grateful for the support and opportunities that had guided me to that point. During high school, I was the number two in the entire college, and at the University, I was inside the small group of the best ones.

"Proudly Carrying the Flag"

In this moment, Debora had the honor of being the flag-bearer at school, a symbol of not only academic excellence but the values of dedication and hard work. Holding her country's flag felt like carrying the hopes of my future.

As I continued to excel academically, my confidence blossomed. I began to realize that with determination, I could achieve anything I set my mind to. A mindset that would prove invaluable as I stepped into the world of technology. My journey as a top student taught me that perseverance and a passion for learning are the keys to unlocking limitless possibilities, shaping a future defined not by boundaries, but by the power of imagination.

These early lessons would become my compass as I ventured into a world traditionally dominated by men. The challenges I faced didn't intimidate me; they fueled my resolve. Each new obstacle was another chance to prove that growth comes from persistence and curiosity. Little did I know, those formative years were not just preparing me to excel academically but also laying the foundation for a career that would push me to break barriers and innovate in ways I could never have imagined.

The Digital Leap – Education and Early Career

Problems, problems, math problems, and numbers.

Numbers have always fascinated me. Their clarity and objectivity stood out in a world where many things, like books, art, or music, could be so subjective. Numbers have an intrinsic value and a universal truth that I found both comforting and intriguing. There was a sense of order and predictability with numbers that gave me a certain peace. While others found math intimidating, for me, it was a language I understood naturally, a constant amidst the chaos of uncertainty.

However, I didn't have a clear vision of what I wanted my professional future to be. The adult version of myself was still a mystery. Without a concrete idea of what would make me happy in my future adult life, I decided to be practical. Since numbers came easily to me and mathematical problems captivated my interest, I pursued engineering. It seemed like an adventure worth embarking on. And I chose it considering the indicator of simplicity; I considered it as a career that would be naturally easy for me so I could spend time playing basketball or working.

What I didn't realize at the time was how this practical decision would open doors to a world of technology and innovation I couldn't have anticipated. The more I delved into engineering, the more I saw its potential not just as a career, but to solve real-world problems, create solutions, and contribute meaningfully to society. It became more than numbers. It became about connecting dots in ways I hadn't imagined, about turning theories into applications, and about the thrill of seeing ideas take shape in the real world.

During the first three years of the different engineering careers inside the engineering university are similar, so I had planned to try software engineering and change to another engineering field if I felt that was not good for me. It was 1994, and at that moment, thinking about what I would do as a software engineer professional in the market wasn't very clear.

One important lesson I've learned and wish to share with you is this: in a life that may span 80 or 100 years, you don't need to define precisely what you want to do when you're 18 years old. You have the freedom to explore, change directions, and pursue multiple careers. You are not limited to a single path, and you are certainly not done learning when you finish your formal education.

The idea that learning is a continuous process can be incredibly relieving, especially in the fast-paced tech industry. Since day one, my journey in technology has been a continuous educational path. With technology constantly evolving, there's always a new coding language to master, a new methodology to adopt, and more computing power to harness for creating sophisticated software. One essential characteristic of the tech world is that knowledge is at your fingertips, and you must be self-motivated to learn. This makes tech professionals quite autodidactic.

When I was at the university, acquiring new technology books was an adventure. I had to order them from a local store, which then sourced them from abroad, resulting in a 3- to 4-week delay. Back then, I preferred learning from physical books, a method that required patience and persistence. Each book that finally arrived felt like a treasured hour of new knowledge waiting to be unlocked. It was a time when learning wasn't just about the information itself but also about the determination to access it.

Fast forward to today, and the landscape of learning has transformed dramatically. We now have podcasts, audiobooks, webinars, and seminars available at our fingertips. Trust me when I say that learning is easier and more accessible now than ever before in history. With just a smartphone, you can explore a world of knowledge. No longer do you have to wait for weeks or hunt down resources, the information you seek is always just a tap away. **The barriers to education have been removed, and the only limit left is your willingness to explore.** So please seize this opportunity. Learn whatever you want, whenever you want, with the tiny device you are holding right now in your hand. The journey to knowledge has never been so quick, so easy, or so exciting.

"My Gateway to Change"

With just this small device, Debora had the power to build solutions, innovate, and change the world for the better. This computer is more than a tool, it's the key to unlocking possibilities and making a lasting impact.

In my first year as a student at the Technological University of my town, my professor of Computing told us:

"You know an Engineer is a human who will use his intelligence to solve problems."

It was the most revealing moment of my career; in a second, he made me think that I could solve any problem that came my way. So suddenly, that gave me the superpower I had always dreamed of having.

Funny, I don't even remember his name, but you know, sometimes the universe sends a message. There were so many issues around me, in my communities, and in my country, all of them waiting for someone intelligent and brave enough to face them. And I am still on that journey.

Every day, I spend time thinking about huge problems to see what great ideas I could come up with to fix or improve them. As an engineer, I would be playing a crucial role in my planet, and it was very clear to me that that was what I wanted to do, but I was not sure If I was capable enough to finish the university, a woman who just finished high school in a School with an educational orientation, and I was there among a lot of boys coming from technical schools ready to be engineers.

When I was 18 years old, I took my first job as a cashier at a local supermarket. I set aside half of my monthly earnings to save up for my first computer, a dream I was eager to make a reality. Working weekends and attending university classes in the afternoon felt like a natural rhythm, and I embraced the structure it brought to my life. At the same time, I was also part of the university basketball team, which kept me grounded and helped me maintain my competitive edge. Balancing work, studies, and basketball was a challenge I welcomed wholeheartedly. The discipline and time management skills I developed during this period came effortlessly, fueling my drive to excel in every aspect of my life.

These years were incredibly busy, yet the constant activity felt right. I thrived on the steady pace of my schedule, finding joy in the balance between work and play. The more I pushed myself, the more I realized my capacity for hard work and the boundless energy propelling me.
During my second year of university, while attending programming classes, an exciting opportunity came my way. I received a job offer from a local software company, which was the next logical step in my journey. With confidence, I left my supermarket job in 1996 and smoothly transitioned into the tech industry, eager to dive into my first role as a software engineer.

One of the most impactful aspects of my early tech career was the incredible mentors I had the privilege of working with. They were extraordinary engineers who were incredibly focused and goal-oriented, setting high standards and pushing boundaries in the projects we undertook. Their expertise and dedication were inspiring and contagious, and their guidance played a pivotal role in shaping my approach to engineering.

This shift marked a significant milestone in my professional life, but it wasn't a daunting leap; it was a natural progression that aligned perfectly with my skills and interests. The experiences and habits I cultivated during my early years set the stage for a successful career where I would continue to grow and thrive.

I finished my degree in 1999, becoming the first person in my family to achieve this milestone. It was a moment of immense pride, but it also marked the beginning of a new chapter in my life. I took some time to reflect on what I wanted to pursue as a professional and an adult. After much contemplation, I realized that staying in my hometown wouldn't help me grow or reach my full potential.

Back then, technology hadn't yet become the global force it is today, and the opportunities in my field were limited in a smaller city. I knew I had to make a bold move if I wanted to develop my skills and chase my professional dreams. So, with a mixture of excitement and trepidation, I decided to leave everything behind: my family, friends, colleagues, and the only home I had ever known. I packed up my clothes, a few cherished books, and my trusty computer, the essentials that would accompany me on my journey to a new city filled with possibilities.

Leaving wasn't easy. It meant saying goodbye to my family, knowing I wouldn't have them nearby for comfort. I was stepping into the unknown, alone, unsure of what lay ahead. But somewhere deep inside, I knew that this was the right decision for my future. It was a leap of faith, one driven by the ambition that burned inside me and the determination to make a mark in the world.

And so, that's how my professional journey began by leaving my comfort zone and diving into the uncertainty. I had no map, no clear path ahead, but I had the belief that I could shape my future.

Inside a Software Innovation Lab

After returning to my home country from a job that took me to live in Panama, I found myself back in Buenos Aires in 2007, reflecting on the incredible journey I had just experienced. While working in Panama as a software designer for the platform responsible for controlling the borders of Guatemala, I was part of a team of expats who quickly became like family. We shared everything from work responsibilities to cultural experiences, creating bonds that transcended our professional roles. This experience taught me the importance of collaboration and camaraderie, setting the stage for the next phase of my career.

Shortly after my return, I received a call from IBM—a company already familiar with my work from a prior project. The woman on the

43

phone detailed a critical and high-profile project that would become a turning point in my career. This call felt like a validation of my skills and a recognition of the unique value I could bring to the team. It was the first time IBM would involve members from Latin America in a laboratory team, and the project's requirements were demanding. Knowing they considered me for such a pivotal role was humbling and exhilarating.

The recruiter said, **"We need the best to be candidates,"** which was music to my ears. It was an opportunity I couldn't pass up. **"Yes, I'll do it,"** I replied, feeling excitement and pride. I was about to help build the first Latin Lab Team, a pioneering spirit that filled me with anticipation and a sense of responsibility, knowing that this initiative could inspire future generations.

The selection process was unlike any I had experienced before. It was rigorous and thorough, the only evaluation I remember so vividly after 15 years. The journey began with an initial interview with local IBM representatives in Argentina. As I prepared for this first step, excitement and nerves filled me. The conversation focused on my past experiences and how they aligned with the project's goals, a critical assessment of my journey and potential.

Following this, I conducted a remote interview with a senior member from IBM in the United States. This was where the evaluation delved into more technical aspects, focusing on architectural application design. I had to articulate my product design philosophies and demonstrate my technical knowledge, a challenge that pushed me to showcase my expertise and adaptability. The questions were challenging, forcing me to think on my feet and communicate my understanding effectively.

After successfully navigating this stage, I was called into the IBM office in Buenos Aires for a series of written tests. These tests assessed various skills, from problem-solving to coding proficiency. I remember sitting in a quiet, structured environment, wholly immersed in the tasks. The intensity of the tests was reminiscent of my university days, yet it felt invigorating. It was a test of not just my technical skills but also my resilience and dedication.

The evaluation continued with additional remote interviews, each testing different aspects of my capabilities, such as management, ability to work within a team, and on my approach to innovation and continuous learning. The questions were varied and often unexpected, requiring me to draw on a wide range of experiences and knowledge. This two-month process was transformative, far more extensive, and diverse than any evaluation I had experienced before.

Throughout this intense process, I remained calm and focused. I wasn't stressed because I believed it would happen if I were meant to be part of this team. My confidence was rooted in the knowledge that I was prepared and ready for whatever came my way. Finally, one day, I received a call confirming my acceptance. That moment felt like being selected to compete on an international stage, representing not just myself but also my community and my country. The sense of achievement was profound, marking the beginning of an exciting new chapter in my career.

Being in the US, the epicenter of technology and innovation, filled Debora with energy and inspiration. Surrounded by groundbreaking ideas, she felt more motivated than ever to push boundaries and shape the future.

I entered my first day at IBM filled with anticipation but unsure of what to expect. Until that morning, I hadn't considered what my colleagues would be like or the specific tasks that awaited me. At 9 AM, I arrived at the IBM building in Buenos Aires, a prominent hub for software services, ready to embark on this new journey.

As I stepped into the office, I was greeted by my new colleagues for the first time. Then, I realized I was the only woman on the Latin team, which comprised three members from Brazil and four from Argentina. This realization added a layer of significance to my role, motivating me to excel and contribute meaningfully to the team.

Moreover, I was the only woman inside the IBM CIO Security Lab, headquartered in New York City and directly under the Vice President of Security's responsibility. The challenges ahead were twofold: not only did I need to establish myself as a woman in tech but also as a Latina working on cutting-edge, global projects.

Without anyone saying a word, I felt an unspoken pressure to prove myself. This pressure came from within. The desire to show that I belonged and excel drove me to push my boundaries and strive for excellence. I needed to demonstrate that I was on par with the rest of the team.

When you find yourself as the sole representative of your gender in a team, it's hard not to feel different. This realization struck my confidence initially, making me question if something was wrong. However, I soon learned to see this situation differently. Instead of feeling out of place, I began to appreciate my unique opportunity. I was where I wanted to be, doing what I loved and bringing a valuable and unique perspective.

I understood that being different wasn't inherently good or bad—it was just different. This perspective allowed me to embrace my uniqueness and see it as a strength rather than a disadvantage. It taught me to be grateful for my chosen path, recognize the value of diversity, and stand confidently in my own identity, knowing that my unique perspective was a valuable asset to the team.

I embraced my "being different" to demonstrate different results, often better ones because I was determined to be a top performer. I was hungry because I had left my city and my family to learn, work in the biggest tech companies, and build an excellent engineering career, while this was just another excellent job opportunity for my male colleagues in their hometown. For me, it was a journey fueled by ambition, self-sacrifice, and a desire to excel on a global stage. Providing the support my family needed was always one of my main goals. This drive pushed me to outperform, innovate, and prove that being different was my greatest asset.

*Keep this in mind: any stereotype anyone can have on you,
you can prove them wrong in a day or two.*

I'd like to share what being on a lab team inside IBM was like. To be representative, I'll say that Labs are the heart of innovation, and in a corporation like this one, they are the motor of the big machine. Being able to be part of the IBM lab was exactly the moment when I truly fell in love with innovation and fully embraced my opportunity to build essential solutions. I believed we could create solutions to change the world; it was only a matter of time and investment in great teams hungry for innovation and change.

So, how did this Lab work? We had a list of security problems exposed inside the company, sourced from internal security controls and FBI incidents related to IBM equipment worldwide. As a Lab member, I had the privilege to review this list and choose, with my mentor, which problems I wanted to tackle to find potential solutions. This setup was precisely how a startup works, but in our case, we were a hub of small tech startups within a massive corporation. It's the best analogy I can find to describe the scale of our relatively small team compared to other product teams in the company, yet with a considerable impact.

Once I selected a problem, I would develop a potential solution and work tirelessly to prove its viability. This process allowed me to innovate and think creatively, knowing that every solution had the potential to impact the company's future direction.

While IBM sold a set of products on the market, all its lab teams were focused on the future, building it with every small lab project. Whether a project ended in a promising product or failed, each effort contributed to the future of technology, paving the way for new ideas and solutions.

With total freedom to ideate and create, we also bore a huge responsibility to present our hypotheses and evaluate our progress weekly. This iterative process ensured we were always moving in the right direction, constantly refining our ideas and solutions.

Being part of the Lab Team made it clear why, until 2009, IBM Corp. reserved lab roles for engineers from developed countries. At that time, Silicon Valley dominated the tech world, and the United States was the leading tech nation, more so than today.

However, this initiative showed promising results under the leadership of Sam Palmisano, our IBM CEO. I never confirmed how this initiative started, but I think budget concerns didn't drive it. Instead, it recognized the importance of diverse thinking, as technology had already shown how crucial it was to include the diverse perspectives of human creators, much like Steve Jobs had demonstrated.

After a few months, our team's success was evident. Our leaders in New York had confidence in our capabilities and proactivity, allowing us to be considered an independent cell of the Lab. Additionally, the manager of Global Business Services for Latin America offered me the position of leader of this team and tasked me with growing the team members and lab projects under the ownership of Latin America.

This was a significant step in my career and an iconic moment where I internalized the concept that we could build the future we wanted to see.

The Web 3 Awakening – Breakthrough Projects

To change the world, you have to know the world

This idea has been a guiding principle throughout my life and career, driving me to explore over 20 countries and collaborate with teams of more than 10 countries. Each journey and interaction have enriched my understanding of our diverse world, revealing the unique tapestry of cultures and ideas that span the globe. Whether navigating cultural nuances or adapting to different work styles, every experience has broadened my perspective and strengthened my belief that innovation thrives in diversity. Actual progress comes from embracing the unique contributions of individuals from all walks of life.

By immersing myself in these varied environments, I've gained insights into worldwide challenges and opportunities, empowering me to create solutions that truly resonate with people's lives. In my quest to change the world, I've discovered that understanding it is the first step, and collaboration across borders is the key to unlocking its potential.

Embracing a Global Perspective

Every project and team I've worked with across different countries has taught me invaluable lessons, reshaping my understanding and expanding my horizons in ways I never imagined. One vivid memory stands out: sitting in an office in Panama City, discussing software solutions with a team from three different countries. Each person brought a unique perspective, transforming a complex problem into an innovative masterpiece.

The beauty of working internationally is the constant learning and adaptation it demands. Cultural diversity brings a wealth of perspectives and approaches to problem-solving, enriching the creative process and leading to more innovative solutions. Whether navigating complex software development issues or understanding the unique needs of different communities, these global experiences have equipped me with the skills and insights necessary to excel in any situation.

Embracing these experiences has not only made me a better software engineer but also a more empathetic and versatile individual. In every aspect of life, from professional endeavors to personal relationships, the lessons learned from working with diverse teams have proven to be invaluable. As I continue my journey, I carry with me the knowledge that every encounter, collaboration, and challenge is an opportunity to learn and grow. The global perspective I've gained is a testament to the power of diversity and the endless possibilities that come with embracing new experiences.

In 1994, I wrote my first algorithms, marking the beginning of a journey through a rapidly evolving technological landscape. As technology progressed, so did my relationship with it. My passion was built on enthusiasm and a high aptitude for developing software applications, and this passion fueled me for many years. My curiosity and desire for growth were continuously fed by emerging technologies and the increasingly complex challenges I faced. However, a more profound need for purpose lingered, quietly waiting for the right moment to take priority.

The first iconic moment in my software-building career came in 2004 when I worked for Telefónica de Argentina, the company responsible for landlines in my country.

At that time, landlines were the primary means of communication for many households, and ensuring their reliability was crucial. If you were a client of the company and had a technical problem with your line, you could call the 118 number from your phone, and this was where our work became vital.

The process behind the support service attending the 118 calls was intricate and essential. It involved creating a technical work order and executing an automatic test over the line to diagnose and address any issues. Our team was tasked with developing a software solution that could handle these tasks efficiently and accurately.

I vividly remember the long hours and the intense brainstorming sessions to ensure the software was robust and user-friendly. We worked through countless challenges, from debugging code to optimizing the system for better performance. Each team member brought unique skills and perspectives, making our collaboration a rich and rewarding experience.

One of the most memorable days was when we finally deployed the software and saw it in action for the first time. The moment of truth came when I called my grandmother to tell her that the software my team and I had created would attend to any issue with her telephone line. Her voice, filled with pride and love, resonated deeply with me. Knowing that our work was directly helping people, especially someone as dear to me as my grandmother, made all the hard work worthwhile.

This experience taught me the importance of placing technology at the service of what people need most. This project was not just about fixing phone lines; it was about connecting people and ensuring they could communicate seamlessly with their loved ones. It was about using technology to solve real-world problems and make a tangible difference. And for me, it was the beginning of a journey filled with many more moments of pride and fulfillment.

Time was passing by, and everything seemed to be improving as the technology I could access grew stronger and more affordable. This ever-evolving tech stack constantly fueled my enthusiasm and ability to innovate.

Then, one day, everything changed. I found myself stuck in my hometown amid a global pandemic. The world was in turmoil, and I spent my days focused on my creativity, studying, and designing solutions. This convergence of circumstances was a turning point, transforming my passion for technology into a profound sense of purpose.

The idea of solving my community's issues through technology, a notion that had been with me since I was young, suddenly became an urgent call to action. The pandemic highlighted the vulnerabilities and challenges we faced, and I felt a deep responsibility to use my expertise to create better opportunities for people in need.

In the midst of global uncertainty and fear, my childhood dream of being a superhero, fighting for justice and equality, reawakened within me. It was no longer just about personal achievement; it was about making a meaningful difference in the lives of others. This realization marked a pivotal moment in my life, where my passion for technology evolved into a mission to help and uplift my community, creating a brighter, more resilient future for us all.

From then on, every project, every innovative idea, and every challenge I faced became more than just a technical pursuit; it became a deliberate effort to make a meaningful difference in people's lives. The experience of living through the COVID pandemic marked a significant turning point in my professional journey.

"Exploring the World to Change It"

As Debora sought to make a difference, she traveled to understand diverse societies, learning from their strengths and challenges.

Empowering Communities

I have known about cryptocurrencies since 2011, but at that moment,

I only saw them as the promise of new digital currencies and an amazing opportunity to create decentralized tech solutions. I had a very technical point of view because I had the knowledge to understand how the network and encryption worked.

However, it was in 2020 that I truly saw how powerful this technology could be in solving problems beyond financial inclusion. The decentralized network model transcended the concept of giving people the power to face their own problems and solve them, generating new businesses and increasing local economies.

As I ventured into the world of Web3, I discovered the transformative power of decentralized technologies and the vibrant community rallying behind the promise of a more equitable digital landscape. Web3, with its decentralized principles, became the catalyst for me to transcend from a mere passion to a purpose-driven mission.

Reflecting on these iconic moments, I realize how they shaped my career and my approach to problem-solving in technology. They reinforced my belief in the power of perseverance, innovation, and collaboration. They also showed me the profound impact our work as software engineers could have on the lives of everyday people.

Additionally, Web3 gave me the opportunity to be involved with amazing communities following dreams, breaking barriers and creating impact on our planet, like-minded beautiful people.

The UN Session

After the pandemic, I decided to fly to the US to attend the NFT NYC event, a pivotal moment in my journey. The energy and innovation of the ecosystem resonated with me deeply, and I realized the immense potential of implementing Web3 solutions that could have a tangible impact on the real world.

There was a missing chain link between my soul calling and my current professional impact in my communities.

During those exciting days, I found myself in a room filled with a group of inspiring Latin American women discussing their Web3 projects, and my connection with them was a perfect flash. That encounter opened the door for me to participate in the 78th UN Science Summit with Women of Web3. From the first moment, it felt like a dream come true that I would treasure forever.

"Redefining Power Through Web3 at the UN"

*Speaking at the UNGA 78th session, Debora shared how Web3
technology is decentralizing power, driven by open communities, and
reshaping the way we collaborate to achieve global impact.*

This opportunity forged a profound connection between my career
aspirations and my desire to work on projects that create meaningful
impact. The experience solidified my commitment to using Web3 as
a force for positive change and contributing to initiatives that empower
communities and drive sustainability.

Building Tomorrow: Current Ventures and Impact

Almost my whole life, I've been a woman in tech, navigating a path
that sometimes felt more challenging than it might for a man. I always
aimed to be the best, striving to be a leader and a differentiator in the
field. Despite the odds, my determination and passion have driven me
to excel as a coder, a tech leader, and eventually a founder. The
honor of achieving these roles fills me with immense happiness,
rendering any minor uncomfortable situations insignificant.

Technology stacks have come and gone in my journey, but they never
held personal significance for me until I encountered Web3. Now, I
find myself at a pivotal moment where solving real-world problems
aligns seamlessly with the philosophical architecture of Web3. The
reduced cost and increased power of current technologies create an

environment ripe for innovation. As a proud woman in Web3, I am dedicated to finding opportunities to leverage this technology to address the most pressing needs of people.

Web3 is not just about technological advancements; it's about using those advancements to create meaningful change. As a woman in Web3, I am driven by a purpose to build solutions that address real-world problems, empower individuals, and foster a sense of community and belonging. The decentralized nature of Web3 aligns perfectly with my vision of a more equitable future where technology serves as a tool for empowerment and progress.

In Web3, I see a chance to lead by example, inspiring other women to join this exciting field and advocating for equal representation and technological opportunities. Together, we can pave the way for a new generation of women in tech, creating a more diverse and inclusive digital landscape that benefits us all.

Leading the Future

Throughout my career, I have been privileged to lead a diverse group of projects, each driven by a distinct vision and purpose. Today, I am deeply involved in three groundbreaking initiatives spanning education, sustainability, and financial freedom. These projects reflect my commitment to leveraging technology for societal impact and represent my dedication to addressing some of the most pressing challenges of our time.

"From Dreams to Leadership"

From the early days of curiosity and potential to becoming a professional leader in technology, this journey has been shaped by growth, learning, and the drive to create a lasting impact.

Web3 for Education: Educational Metaverse for Kids

One of the projects I am leading is the development of an educational metaverse for children in Colombia. This initiative is designed to offer a dynamic and immersive learning experience where young minds can explore the world through the lens of human rights. By navigating virtual cities that symbolize our shared rights and history, students will gain a deeper understanding of these fundamental principles in a way that is both engaging and impactful.

This project is particularly close to my heart because of my commitment to education and my desire to give back to the community that supported me throughout my educational journey. Public education played a pivotal role in shaping who I am today, and this initiative is my way of extending that gift to the next generation. We aim to make learning about human rights accessible and meaningful, empowering children to become informed global citizens and advocates for positive change.

The power of the metaverse allows us to create immersive learning experiences that enable children to travel around the world without leaving their classrooms. This technology, though still in its early stages, is one of the most powerful tools we have today. It can transport students into meticulously replicated versions of international cities or immerse them in civilizations of the past, providing a unique and engaging educational experience that goes beyond traditional methods. By exploring these digital worlds, students can gain a deeper understanding of history, culture, and geography, making learning both exciting and impactful.

My vision is to create a platform where education is not confined by the limitations of the physical world. Through the metaverse, we can inspire a new generation of learners to dream bigger and reach higher. We want to equip them with the knowledge and tools necessary to make a meaningful impact in their communities and beyond. In doing so, I hope to contribute to a future where human rights are universally respected and upheld.

Web3 for Sustainability: Cleaning the Rio Torres in Costa Rica with NFT Funding

The **Rio Torres**, a major river in Costa Rica, has been plagued by pollution for years, severely impacting the environment and local communities. Today, I am leading an innovative project that combines cutting-edge technology with environmental activism to recover and revitalize this vital waterway.

When I was approached to design a proposal for this project, I immediately saw it as a perfect opportunity to use my skills to make a meaningful impact. Water management is in my DNA; growing up in a desert region, I have long been accustomed to tackling water emergencies. This personal connection fueled my passion to find a solution for the Rio Torres, which has become a symbol of hope and renewal for the people of Costa Rica.

The challenge was to create a Web3 technology strategy that would raise funds and build a global community passionate about sustainability. Our innovative solution involves using **NFTs for Good** (Non-Fungible Tokens) as a means of funding the restoration of the Rio Torres. This approach allows people worldwide to support the cause while owning unique digital assets that represent their commitment to environmental stewardship.

By creating a decentralized fundraising platform, we can overcome traditional barriers and engage a diverse audience eager to contribute to positive change. These NFTs are more than just digital collectibles; they are symbols of a global movement to preserve our planet's most precious resource.

What makes this initiative genuinely unique is its combination of technology, creativity, and social responsibility. We have crafted a sustainable model that addresses a pressing environmental issue while showcasing how Web3 technologies can be leveraged for good.

This project is a testament to the power of innovation and collaboration in tackling global challenges. It serves as a shining example of how we can use modern tools to create tangible impact and foster a sense of community across borders.

I hope this project will be the first of many related to water cleaning and management. By demonstrating the effectiveness of our approach, we aim to inspire similar initiatives worldwide, proving that technology can be a powerful ally in the fight for a cleaner, more sustainable planet.

Through this project, I am reminded of the immense potential we have when we unite for a common cause.

Web3 for Financial Freedom: R3al Blocks RWA Tokenization Platform

I founded R3al Blocks, a real-world asset tokenization platform dedicated to breaking down barriers to property ownership in Latin America. Our mission is to democratize access to private property by leveraging the power of Web3 technology. And just like this sounds, it is the hardest job I ever had.

In many parts of Latin America, access to credit is a significant obstacle to property ownership. This challenge prevents countless individuals from owning their own homes or cars, or small businesses. At R3al Blocks, we see Web3 as a catalyst for change, enabling us to create innovative solutions that address this issue head-on.

We can fractionalize assets through tokenization, dividing them into smaller, more affordable units. This approach allows us to offer property ownership opportunities to a broader audience, enabling individuals to invest in small pieces of an asset with minimal financial barriers. Our platform empowers people by giving them access to real estate investments that were previously out of reach. Utilizing blockchain technology ensures transparency, security, and accessibility for all users, making the dream of property ownership a reality for many.

As we navigate and overcome each obstacle, we are determined to create thousands of new property owners this year. Our commitment to innovation and inclusivity drives us forward, and we are excited to witness the transformative impact of our efforts on individuals and communities across Latin America. With R3al Blocks, we are not just building a business; we are building a movement towards financial freedom and empowerment. Our platform is a testament to the potential of Web3 technology to create meaningful change, and we are proud to be at the forefront of this exciting revolution.

Looking Ahead – Future Aspirations

As with any new technology, Web3 is poised to move forward into a maturity phase, becoming a seamless part of our daily lives. The complex fog that currently surrounds it will dissipate, allowing a broader audience to access its benefits. It will become natural for us to use decentralized apps for everything from banking to education, and tokenized assets will be woven into the fabric of our jobs and daily functions.

I envision a future where a humanity-centered design approach drives sustainability and financial solutions. Web3 is not just a technological advancement but a catalyst for addressing some of our most significant sustainable challenges. It offers one of our greatest hopes for a better, more equitable world.

Imagine a world where tokenization and community empowerment work hand in hand to drive the change we desperately need. Through blockchain technology, communities can take ownership of their resources and drive initiatives that reflect on their unique needs and values. This transformation is not just theoretical; it is actionable and achievable.

I am committed to leading this change. My focus will remain on sustainability and financial freedom, leveraging the power of Web3 to create solutions that benefit people and the planet. I aim to collaborate with diverse teams to explore innovative ideas, drive adoption, and influence the growth of ethical technology.

In the future, I see myself as an active member of committees or companies fully dedicated to the evaluation and implementation of solutions and legislation for a brighter future. Whether it's contributing to policy-making or mentoring young women in tech, my role will be to inspire and guide others on their tech journeys.

As I conclude this chapter of my life and career, I am filled with hope and excitement for what lies ahead. My journey as a woman in tech and Web3 has been challenging but rewarding, and it is far from over. I look forward to continuing to break down barriers, shatter stereotypes, and make a lasting impact on the world.

Conclusion

Throughout my journey, I've learned that your determination and consistency are the most powerful tools you need to follow your dreams and create the life you envision. Never let your circumstances, country, gender, or social class define or limit you.

You can achieve anything you set your mind to, no matter where you start.Believe in yourself and make decisions based on your hopes, not your fears. Every challenge you face is an opportunity for growth and transformation. Remember, the path to your dreams is paved with courage, persistence, and resilience. I urge you to embrace your passions, pursue your goals relentlessly, and never lose sight of the potential within you. You have the power to shape your future and inspire others along the way.

Go out and create the future you desire. The world is waiting for your unique contribution.

Reflection

As Steve Jobs so wisely said, "Everything around you that you call life was made up by people that were no smarter than you, and you can change it, you can influence it, you can build your own things that other people can use."

If you've reached this part of my story and feel even a tiny spark of curiosity or wonder about what it would be like to be a woman in technology, **follow it.** You owe it to yourself to see what could unfold if you just **give it a try**.

The world of technology is vast, but within it lies something incredibly profound: **the power to create.** When we step into this field, we aren't just part of an industry we are **creators**, shaping the future in real-time. We build products and services that solve problems, connect people, and transform the way we live, work, and interact. We don't just adapt to change, we drive it.

Technology is not just about coding, algorithms, or data. It's about **creativity**, **imagination**, and **vision**. It's about using these tools to build a better tomorrow for yourself, your community, and generations to come. This is why I fell in love with technology: because of its unlimited potential to transform lives and create impact in ways we can't always foresee.

But here's the thing: you don't have to be the best at math, have the perfect background, or know exactly where you're going to succeed. You need the courage to start, the willingness to learn, and the determination to keep going. Your perspective, your voice, your ideas these are **powerful**. And this world, especially the tech world, needs **more women** like you. Women who see things differently. Women who are ready to break barriers, create change, and lead with both intellect and heart. I want to leave you with one final thought:

Embrace your power. Embrace your uniqueness.

You can shape not only your future but transform entire communities and, ultimately, the world. Technology gives us the tools, but **you** bring the vision. Every day, with every choice you make, you decide what kind of world we'll live in. Don't wait for someone else to build that world for you. **Build it yourself.**

The future is in your hands. And trust me, it's brighter than you can imagine. <3

With gratitude, Deb Carrizo.

Let's Connect

Débora Betsabé Mercedes Carrizo
www.womenofweb3un.io/speakers/debora-carrizo

CHAPTER THREE

From Survival to Advocacy:
A Journey of Resilience and Innovation
By Marisa "Ritzy P" Estrada Rivera

From the streets of South Bay San Diego, where I navigated the challenges of being a first-generation Mexican-American, to speaking at the United Nations, my journey has been one of survival, discovery, and advocacy.

Undercover Nerd: I Was Just Worried About Survival

As a first-generation Mexican-American born to a single mom and raised two exits from the Mexican border in South Bay San Diego, most of my life was about survival. Though Spanish was my first language, growing up in the early 80s meant it was discouraged to speak Spanish at school. Learning English early was my ticket to success in this new world.

The elementary school I attended was predominantly Latino and Filipino. In third grade, it was discovered that I was an advanced student, excelling in reading. The top reading group consisted of two boys and me. It was mentioned that we were all going to skip a grade. I'm not sure if the paperwork ever reached my mom, but I didn't end up advancing, though Nomer and Rudy did. Yes, I still remember their names. I didn't have anyone advocating for me.

Marisa "Ritzy P" presenting at the 2024 Ambies Awards, Los Angeles, CA.

Marisa "Ritzy P" childhood photos

Access to STEAM During My Formative Years in the Early 80s

Computers: I can count on my hands the few times our class was allowed to visit the computer lab to learn the new programming language, LOGO. We would type in commands to direct the "turtle" to move and draw shapes. It felt underwhelming. No one took the time to explain what it was or its potential applications. At the time, I didn't understand what data was, but I knew I needed more of it. Why should I learn something when owning a computer was out of reach for me? Our school could barely afford them, let alone individual students.

Logo Programming Language from the 1980's

Space: I remember being in the library the morning of January 28th, 1986. I was 11, in 6th grade. We were all excited to witness a woman become the first teacher to fly into space on the space shuttle Challenger. What we ended up witnessing was a horrific tragedy that left us stunned, shocked, afraid, and confused. There was no support afterward; we rarely spoke of it.

Science: I can't recall any notable science projects or programs. While others eyed the latest toys or gadgets as rewards for their achievements, I secretly chose a microscope when I hit my Girl Scout Cookie sales goals (Troop 713). I spent hours examining brine shrimp eggs that came with the kit and anything else that sparked my curiosity under that microscope. I still have that microscope today.

Space Shuttle Challenger Crew Left: STS-51L crew members Michael J. Smith, front row left, Francis R. "Dick" Scobee, Ronald E. McNair; Ellison S. Onizuka, back row left, S. Christa McAuliffe, Gregory B. Jarvis, and Judith A. Resnik.

During my elementary years, school was my escape from a traumatic home life. I was serious about being curious, but the constraints of the antiquated school system left me bored. I had a thirst for knowledge, which would serve me well later in life.

From Honors to Gen Pop: A Strategic Exit from Advanced Classes

When I entered 7th grade, I was placed in honor classes since I was highly advanced academically. This meant I had several classes with the same students. Simultaneously, my home life intensified, and I was just trying to survive. I didn't have the support or bandwidth to be excited about intense debates and group projects, and I didn't want to look like the nerd I was. Adding hormones to the mix, I was not in the best place mentally. I had no one advocating for me and lacked the foresight to see the long-term benefits of staying in honors. After two years of honors classes, I, as my mom's translator, explained to her that I needed her signature for school. I didn't mention that it was to remove me from those classes. If she had known what was at stake, she would never have signed the forms. I returned to gen pop, aka general population.

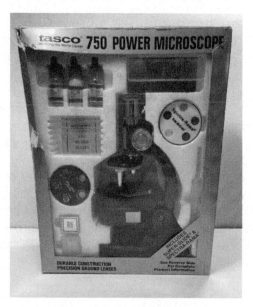

Marisa "Ritzy P" 's Tasco Microscope she won in elementary school.

I ended up transferring after my sophomore year to another high school, one focused on visual and performing arts. Art didn't seem like a viable path for someone from our community, but I knew I was an artist at heart, even if I didn't fit the stereotype. I didn't sketch or paint daily; instead, I was trying to navigate a world that didn't always seem welcoming. I excelled in my art, choir, and dance performances, but I still didn't know what I wanted to do with my life.

During my junior year, my mom was diagnosed with breast cancer. She was my only supporter, my world, and now she was dying. Those last years of high school were a blur. I didn't have anyone to talk to about what I was going through, let alone anyone to help me figure out what I would do after high school.

It wasn't until a field trip to a design firm, where the founder explained that design was a fusion of art, communication, and emerging technology—at the beginning of computer-aided design—that things clicked for me. Suddenly, integrating ART into STEM education to create STEAM made sense. It was an opportunity for my creative and analytical sides to collaborate, prompting me to explore the critical role of art in technology.

Academic Background and Non-Linear Career Path

Once I saw how graphic design blended my love of art, design, and tech, I found what I wanted to do—become a graphic designer. During the earlier mentioned field trip to the design firm, the founder told me that if I couldn't afford the famed ArtCenter College of Design in Pasadena, California, then California State University Long Beach was the next best thing at a fraction of the cost. They have one of the best design programs. Since it seemed I was overlooked by the guidance counselors in high school, I had to do my own research on how to apply. I was accepted but couldn't afford tuition, so for the first two years, I attended San Diego Community College full-time and worked full-time until 11 pm at the local private airport. Eventually, I transferred to California State University Long Beach to pursue a bachelor's in art with an emphasis in graphic design and marketing.

Marisa "Ritzy P" 's High School Graduation photo

When I moved, my mother's breast cancer was in remission. Sadly, during my first year at California State University Long Beach, her cancer returned, and she passed away on April 13th, 1995. Being the first in my family to attend college, I promised her that no matter what, I would graduate. I found myself navigating the world alone, taking out several loans and working tirelessly. It was a challenging journey, but I fulfilled that promise, graduating two years later. Armed with a degree and a commitment to my late mother, I entered the vibrant and tumultuous world of the music industry.

Marisa "Ritzy P" with her mama as a child and as a young adult

In my early roles in the industry—working as an independent radio promotions person, Hits Magazine, House of Blues Concerts, and AEG Live Presents—I quickly discovered my knack for connecting, curating, and creative marketing. There were hardly any women in the industry, and few who looked like me. As usual, women were overworked and underpaid, but I found a community and made it work.

However, my last full-time role in the music industry as a print buyer/production manager became overwhelming, with ad buys matching my yearly salary and navigating the demands of challenging artist egos. Feeling the need for more meaningful work, I gave my four-month notice and launched Ritzy Periwinkle in 2006. This allowed me to pursue creative endeavors that felt more fulfilling and purposeful compared to my previous role in the music industry.

Marisa "Ritzy P" painting along with photos of various art pieces.

During this time, I also began exhibiting as a multidisciplinary artist in Los Angeles, spent two consecutive years at Art Basel Miami for exhibitions and painting murals, and expanded internationally. Exhibiting internationally allowed me to reach new audiences, collaborate with diverse artists, and explore different cultural influences, all of which enriched my artistic practice and expanded my professional network.

In 2009, I ventured into the designer vinyl toy world, debuting at San Diego Comic Con with releases and signings. This led me to connect with artists worldwide. In 2011, I combined my art with philanthropy, embarking on a month-long tour of Southeast Asia that began with a two-week stint with refugee children at the Thai-Burmese border. Using art as therapy, we communicated through creativity. This tour was made possible by leveraging the internet and community to raise funds and awareness. Documentaries such as 'Little Lotus Project' by Spinning Top and 'Paint Life' by Daniel Zana captured this journey, solidifying my commitment to global humanitarian efforts.

Marisa "Ritzy P" in Maesot, Thailand helping the students paint a mural at their school.

As a solopreneur, I focused on creative direction and brand strategy for major corporations while also working artist relations for major music festivals, Coachella and Stagecoach, for over seven years. During this time, I observed the increasing integration of art in various forms with technology across our world.

Fast forward to 2020, I had the honor of speaking at Wonder Women Tech on 'Creativity, Technology, and Legacy.' This opportunity allowed me to connect the dots between my passion for creativity and technology, emphasizing their combined impact.

How I entered Web3

I owe it all to a podcast episode, Twitter/X Space, and a Google meeting. Let me explain.

2020 was about to be an amazing year for both my husband and me. We work for ourselves, and most of our clients were in live music and live events. In January 2020, I had just come off working on the Land Rover 4xFAR fest. Then the pandemic hit, and we immediately had to pivot, but pivot to what?

So, I did what many of us did: found clients in other industries, took on projects I swore I would never do, and worked on projects at severely discounted prices to provide for our family during those uncertain times.

In early 2021, one of my internationally known artist friends, Sket One, who happens to be a white male, mentioned he was launching NFTs. He didn't fully grasp what they were, relying on a company for guidance. Intrigued, my friends and I asked, 'What are NFTs?' That sparked my deep dive into research, opening the door to Web3 and a whole new world. I immersed myself in learning—I nerded out, you know, when you discover something and want to understand everything about it.

Left: Word to Your Mama Podcast cover art. Right: The Tim Ferris Show Podcast cover art.

Before the pandemic, I was already an avid podcast listener, but during lockdowns, I found myself tuning in even more. In fall 2020, I even launched my own podcast, *Word To Your Mama*, aimed at amplifying diverse voices from the music, art, and emerging tech industries. In October 2021, I came across an episode of The Tim Ferris Show titled *#542: Chris Dixon and Naval Ravikant: The Wonders of Web3, How to Pick the Right Hill to Climb, Finding the Right Amount of Crypto Regulation, Friends with Benefits, and the Untapped Potential of NFTs*. Spanning 2 hours and 31 minutes, I broke it into parts and listened while cooking and cleaning. They broke down Web1, Web2, and Web3, discussed the potential, and got into DAOs (Decentralized Autonomous Organizations). I was now inspired and intrigued.

One day soon after, I joined my very first Twitter/X Space. It was Latinos discussing Web3. I asked who the Chris Dixons and Naval Ravikants of the Latin@ world were. One of the guys in the Twitter

Space, Oszie Tarula, shared his idea for a Web3 educational and community-building event called Hola Metaverso—something smaller than the regular convention that would allow more opportunities to build. He asked how he should go about finding his team.

Fast forward, he invited a few of us to join his Google meeting to share the deck of his idea. I joined that meeting and found myself the only woman there—it was all Latino men. I thought, "Oh great, tech bros. Even worse, Latino tech bros?" I was totally generalizing and stereotyping. But I still stuck around to be nice. However, I was pleasantly surprised at Oszie's vision for Hola Metaverso; from the start, women were front and center—not just a few token women for the event.

I learn by doing. I wanted to learn as much as possible so that I could make an informed decision on how to properly enter the space with a new business and my art. So, I said yes to being a part of the team to bring our vision of an IRL and virtual Web3 educational and community-building event to life. We started planning via Google meetings and Twitter/X Spaces in January 2022 and had our first Hola Metaverso event in Los Angeles that April.

We were seeing Web3 events in LA that didn't reflect the city on stage, and the tickets were outrageously priced. So, we created an event for around 250 attendees that was inviting and inclusive, featuring VCs, builders, and creators. We wanted everyone to feel welcome and ensured that women speakers were not tokens but leaders in the space.

The event was streamed live globally. Tickets were reasonably priced, and scholarships were available for those who wanted to attend but didn't have the funds. Midway through the event, a young Black gentleman came up to me, hugged me, and said, 'Thank you so much, Ritzy. I was at a Web3 event earlier this month in Malibu and left because I didn't feel welcome. I feel welcome here.' Towards the end of the event, a young Latina woman thanked me, saying she learned a lot and was leaving inspired.

Photos of various Hola Metaverso events.

Since then, we've held events in the US and LATAM—in LA, NYC, Miami, CDMX, Bogotá, and Medellín. As a curator and organizer, I strive to create well-rounded events with diverse speakers. It is about building community. Through this work, I've connected with individuals and organizations utilizing emerging tech. I've seen their work firsthand and I'm a holder and supporter of their efforts.

It became even more clear how emerging tech has the potential to significantly impact industries, economies, and societies. Tech that changes the game—revolutionary stuff.

Back in 1983, when the internet was invented, it wasn't built by us, it wasn't built for us, we weren't even considered. By *us*, I mean marginalized communities. Now, in the span of 41 years, we have gone through three iterations of the internet, spawning much of the emerging tech we see today. We have an opportunity to change things, to be the ones building and creating new solutions with this new technology. Being part of the ecosystem, I connected and cultivated relationships with people whose missions aligned with mine. I knew my mission was to be an advocate for diversity in emerging tech.

As an advocate for marginalized communities, I believe it's crucial for us to occupy spaces in a world that's increasingly tech-centric. Since 2021, I've collaborated with and supported projects that leverage emerging tech to empower marginalized groups socially, creatively, and economically. This dedication led me to incredible opportunities to speak at events such as NFT.NYC and Wonder Women Tech, and in September of 2023, I had the honor of speaking at the United Nations General Assembly 78th Science Summit on the Importance of Diversity in Emerging Tech with the Women of Web3, founded by Sandy Martinez, M.Ed. Because of Sandy and Cyndi Coon, I am writing this chapter in this book. Gracias ladies.

Women of Web3 UNGA78 Photoshoot, September 2023 NYC

All of this was made possible due to community, connection, and building bridges. Genuine, authentic relationships will always win, no matter what industry.

Industries I have been a part of:

- Music
- Design/Visual art
- Customizing vinyl toys and sculptures
- Emerging tech
- Podcasting

Your word is bond, and folks can see how you move.

From the initial steps of survival to standing at the forefront of technological advocacy, my journey has come full circle. I strive to be the advocate I never had growing up. Continuing to champion diversity in emerging tech, I am reminded that our voices, stories, and innovations shape the future.

Current Projects

Partner in Hola Metaverso
Hola Metaverso has held events in over 10 cities internationally. In 2024, we hosted an event the day before VeeCon in Los Angeles, focusing on how U.S. Latinos are driving business and emerging tech. This event connected leaders, investors, developers, and founders. Additionally, we organized our second annual Futurista event in partnership with the University of Medellin, Colombia.

Member of the National Policy Network of Women of Color in Blockchain
This year marks the 5th delegation meeting with policymakers on Capitol Hill in Washington, DC, where we advocate for inclusive blockchain policies.

Member of Women of Web3
We continue to take up space and ensure women and other marginalized communities are part of this transformative ecosystem.

Diversity in Emerging Tech Advocate
I travel internationally to speak on the importance of diversity in emerging tech. I speak to those currently in the industry and, more importantly, to those outside of it, highlighting the importance of staying informed. This year alone, I have spoken at numerous prestigious events, including NFT.NYC, Consensus, Hustle + Socialize, VeeCon, The DNC and many more.

Host of Emerging Tech Journeys Podcast
Through this podcast, we amplify diverse voices in emerging tech. It is geared towards those not currently in the industry; aiming to help them see themselves in this space, understand others' motivations, and hopefully be inspired to join.

Co-Host of *The Get Down* by Butterscotch Media
We delve into policy, industry trends, market research, and their impacts on Black, Latin@s, and Indigenous DeFi retail investors, Web3 consumers, founders, executives, and officials. Our upcoming

events include a Pre-DNC Chicago fireside chat and live podcast taping with policymakers, as well as attending the convention floor as press.

Contributor to the Crypto Council for Innovation and W.K. Kellogg Foundation's Report

I contributed to the report entitled "Building a More Inclusive Web3," a study exploring the potential within the Web3 ecosystem. This ethnographic study provides actionable insights into how Web3 fosters empowerment and financial inclusivity for underrepresented builders.

Marisa "Ritzy P" at various speaking engagements

Why This Work is So Important

The tech industry has a significant diversity gap:

- 35% of tech workers are people of color
- 26% of tech workers are women
- Less than 10% are women of color

Representation is even lower in emerging tech fields like blockchain, artificial intelligence (AI), and the spatial web (AR, VR). Meta, the owner of Facebook, Instagram, WhatsApp, Threads, and Meta Quest, recently formed an AI advisory group. Unfortunately, it is composed entirely of white men, which is concerning but not surprising.

Meta AI Advisory group: Charlie Songhurst, Nat Friedman, Tobi Lütke, Patrick Collison

This lack of diversity is alarming because AI, if developed without input from our communities, can perpetuate existing gender and racial biases. It is crucial that we are represented in these spaces to ensure that technology benefits everyone and addresses the needs and concerns of all communities.

Diversity in tech isn't just a buzzword; it's essential for building fairer, more inclusive technologies and ecosystems. Research has consistently shown that diverse teams drive innovation and outperform homogenous ones. Additionally, embracing diversity in tech leads to financial gains, as diverse companies are more likely to attract top talent, foster innovation, and capture new markets.

Lessons Learned and Paths Forward

As I reflect on my journey; it becomes clear that every step has been guided by a deep-seated belief in the power of diversity and the transformative potential of emerging technologies. From my early days navigating the music industry to founding Ritzy Periwinkle and becoming a multidisciplinary artist, each experience has shaped my path toward advocacy in the Web3 space.

The challenges I've faced—financial hurdles in college, navigating male-dominated industries, and questioning the status quo—have fueled a relentless pursuit of meaningful work. Transitioning into the world of emerging tech, I have found purpose in advocating for marginalized communities, ensuring that our voices are not just heard but actively included in the dialogue shaping our technological future.

Looking ahead, my commitment remains unwavering. I am dedicated to fostering genuine connections and building bridges across communities, believing deeply in the transformative power of diverse perspectives. Through platforms like the Emerging Tech Journeys

Podcast and The Get Down, I aim to amplify voices that are often overlooked and champion initiatives that empower underrepresented groups.

My story serves as a reminder to upcoming innovators in the Web3 space: embrace diversity, forge authentic relationships, pursue meaningful endeavors, and see challenges as opportunities for growth. Together, we can harness the potential of emerging technologies to create a future where inclusivity and innovation go hand in hand, shaping a world that truly reflects the diversity of its inhabitants.

Empowerment Through Innovation: A Personal Mission

During Women's History Month this year, I attended a conference where legendary arts and culture activist Debora Padilla quoted a line that I will never forget.

"If you're not at the table, you're on the menu."

So why emerging tech? It's not just about innovation; it's about shaping a future where everyone has a seat at the table, where technology reflects the rich tapestry of human experience, and where diversity isn't just celebrated but embedded in every aspect. It's about building a better world.

I share my story of survival and my non-linear career path to be the representation I wish I had as a young girl back in San Diego in the '80s. Sometimes, tragedies in life can be gifts. Losing my mom when I was 20 taught me that life is short, and I want to live a life where I add to this world. I do this work for my son, for our community, for all the young girls navigating their paths, and for other marginalized communities globally.

I AM MY ANCESTORS' VENGEANCE

YOU ARE YOUR ANCESTORS' VENGEANCE

Together, let's build a community where innovation is inclusive, and diverse perspectives drive meaningful change in technology. If you're passionate about diversity in tech or have ideas for collaboration, I'd love to hear from you. Feel free to connect with me via email at info@ritzyperiwinkle.com.

Who's with me?

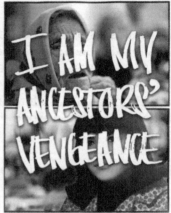

I AM MY ANCESTORS' VENGEANCE NFT, Top is Ritzy's abuelita, Sipriana Rivera. Bottom is Ritzy's mom, Consuelo Rivera.

Let's Connect

Marisa "Ritzy P" Estrada Rivera
www.womenofweb3un.io/speakers/marisa-estrada
@ritzyp on all socials | ritzyperiwinkle.com

CHAPTER FOUR

From Corporate Corridors to Crypto Frontlines
By Leslie Motta

My journey from the corporate corridors of real estate and banking to becoming the COO of one of the most influential media companies in the crypto space—Gokhshtein Media—has been a ride of endless learning, innovation, and personal growth. It's been a journey of discovering new possibilities, like when I founded the Women of Basketball (WOB) project. WOB's mission is close to my heart: to financially support junior college female basketball athletes by filling the gaps that scholarships leave behind. Beyond just funding, it's about shining a light on the challenges these young women face and doing our part to ease their burdens.to space, every step has been a chapter in a larger story of transformation.

My career began in traditional industries—banking and real estate—where I held various roles, always pushing myself to learn and grow. Along the way, I started hosting spaces on X (formerly known as Twitter), creating a platform for women to share their stories and empower each other. I also hosted "Unscripted" with Gokhshtein Media, where I helped bring credible, thought-provoking content to the ever-changing world of blockchain and Web3. Through these roles, I've had the privilege of informing, inspiring, and empowering countless others, all while driving innovative campaigns and building communities.

Livestream of "Unscripted" wrapping up Bitcoin Nashville, TN 2024.

But my journey is far from over. I'm driven by a vision to continue empowering women in the blockchain realm, supporting JUCO female athletes, and building a billion-dollar media company that stands at the forefront of this revolutionary space.

As I reflect on the journey that led me to Gokhshtein Media and the creation of the Women of Basketball project, I realize that it all began long before I entered the corporate world. The seeds of resilience, determination, and a deep sense of purpose were sown during my early years, growing up in a small border town in Arizona. To truly understand the drive behind my work, one must first understand the roots that shaped me.

The Digital Leap

Growing up in a small border town in Arizona, my early years were marked by a blend of cultural richness and economic hardship. As the daughter of Mexican immigrants, I was raised in a single-parent household where my mother was the bedrock of our family. Her strength and resilience were the cornerstones of our upbringing, teaching us that adversity is not a barrier but a steppingstone to greater heights. Her unwavering faith and determination instilled in me the belief that no dream is too distant if pursued with passion and perseverance.

Life's challenges were numerous, growing up with two sisters and a brother, we learned to adapt to our situation. We didn't have much, but we made do with what we had. Sports and music were our outlets—I played the violin in the orchestra—but even then, we had to get creative. Life wasn't easy, but it shaped us into who we are today. From financial struggles to the absence of resources for extracurricular activities, our family learned to adapt and overcome. Despite these obstacles, we found ways to participate in sports and music, borrowing instruments and fundraising to make things work. These experiences fostered a sense of resourcefulness and grit that would serve me well in my future endeavors.

My journey took an unexpected turn when I became a teenage mother. It wasn't part of the plan, but it became part of my story. I finished high school, got married, and moved across states to build a family. I have three amazing children who are now carving out their own paths in life. Becoming a teenage mother and marrying young presented its own set of challenges, but these experiences only reinforced my belief in the power of resilience and adaptability. Though their father and I eventually divorced, I learned that life is full of shifts and changes, and sometimes we have to pivot towards a new journey.

Navigating these trials taught me valuable lessons about the importance of faith and perseverance in the face of adversity. I firmly believe that life's unexpected turns often lead to new opportunities, and that the trials we face are integral to shaping our character and destiny.

I've come to believe that every trial and tribulation prepares us for the greatness we're destined for, and that every closed door is just the beginning of a new chapter. My faith in God and the conviction that every setback is a setup for a comeback have been guiding lights throughout my journey.

When I first encountered the world of Web3, blockchain, and

cryptocurrency, it felt like stepping into a completely new realm. I didn't fully understand it at first, but I knew it held something powerful—a potential for change and innovation that I was drawn to. During my time in real estate and corporate banking, I witnessed the transformative power of technology in facilitating transactions and connecting people across the globe. Yet, it wasn't until much later that I would fully immerse myself in this space.

My expedition into the world of blockchain was like stepping into a new universe. Initially daunting, it soon revealed itself as a realm of endless possibilities. My early experiences in technology, influenced by my ex-spouse's work in the tech field, kindled a fascination that lay dormant until I encountered Bitcoin and the world of blockchain. Despite skepticism and advice to dismiss it as a fleeting trend, the evolution of blockchain technology captivated me.

A pivotal moment came when I reconnected with a dear friend, Brenda Gentry—affectionately known as "Ms. Crypto Mom"— transitioned from banking to embrace cryptocurrency. Her leap of faith inspired me to delve deeper into the Web3 space. When she left the banking world to dive headfirst into crypto, I knew something big was happening. She guided me, shared her knowledge, and soon I found myself immersed in the world of NFTs and Web3. I started participating in spaces on X, listening to founders and innovators, and the more I learned, the more intrigued I became.

It was during this time that my daughter was in her senior year of high school, being recruited to play college basketball. A visit to a junior college in Washington opened my eyes to the harsh realities these young women face—how underfunded and under-resourced they are. I knew I had to do something, and that's how the Women of Basketball project was born.

In 2022, I founded Women of Basketball, an NFT for basketball lovers and donors, to support female athletes at the junior college level. Many of these players juggle multiple jobs just to make ends meet, and scholarships don't always cover everything. For some of these girls, this is their last chance to chase their dream, and I wanted to give them every opportunity to succeed.

While the project has faced its challenges, we've raised funds and are set to make our first donation in September 2024. By the time this book is in your hands, that dream will have become a reality. This is just the beginning of what I hope will be a long journey of giving back, empowering others, and making a difference in this exciting new world.

The lessons of resourcefulness and grit that I learned in my childhood would serve me well as I navigated the complexities of adulthood. Becoming a teenage mother and managing the demands of family life while pursuing a career in banking and real estate was no easy feat. Yet, it was these very experiences that prepared me for the challenges ahead, especially as I began to explore new opportunities in the digital world.

Balancing Dreams and Reality

Building a family meant putting my educational aspirations on hold, but my pursuit of knowledge did not die down. When my children were old enough, I resumed my studies at the University of the Incarnate Word, working towards a Bachelor of Science in Business Administration with a focus on project management. Although life circumstances led me to pause my studies just six classes shy of graduation, I never let that define me. Instead, I focused on honing my skills, earning certifications in Six Sigma, and embracing leadership opportunities that helped shape my career.

I was drawn to project management because it embodied the values that had guided me throughout my life—organization, leadership, and the ability to turn visions into reality. My early career was a blend of traditional roles in real estate and banking, where I developed a strong foundation in business operations, leading teams, and client relations. But I always felt there was something more out there, a space where I could combine my passion for technology, my desire to innovate, and my commitment to making a positive impact.

It was during this time that I began to explore the world of cryptocurrency and blockchain. What started as a curiosity quickly grew into a passion as I realized the transformative potential of this technology. Blockchain was more than just a new financial system; it was a paradigm shift, a way to empower individuals, disrupt traditional industries, and create new opportunities for those who had been left behind by the old system.

The Role of Mentorship in Navigating Web3

Throughout my journey, I have been blessed with mentors who saw potential in me and encouraged me to push beyond my perceived limitations. These mentors were instrumental in helping me navigate the corporate world, teaching me the importance of strategic thinking, effective communication, and the value of building strong, authentic relationships.

Entering the Web3 space was a leap into the unknown, but the support I received from figures like Stacky Robinson was instrumental. Her guidance in navigating blockchain's intricacies, from setting up wallets to trading cryptocurrencies, was a lifeline. With her help and introducing me to David Gokhshtein, I embarked on a journey that would redefine my career and broaden my horizons.

Leslie joined the Gokhshtein Media team to cover the 2024 Karate Combat fight in Nashville, TN. This photo was captured by the pit just before the fight began.

One of the most significant influences in my career has been David Gokhshtein, the CEO and Founder of Gokhshtein Media. His mentorship allowed me to grow within the company, taking on roles that I never imagined I would be qualified for, ultimately leading to my current position as COO. David has been instrumental in helping me build and refine my brand, and together, we have worked to expand the reach and impact of Gokhshtein Media within and outside of the blockchain space. His mentorship has been a cornerstone of my professional development.

My current role at Gokhshtein Media, where I began as a content creator and ascended to the position of Chief Operating Officer, is a testament to the guidance and support I received from David. His belief in my potential, coupled with the skills I honed through public speaking and corporate training, empowered me to navigate the complexities of managing a media company in the blockchain space.

For a long time, I felt unqualified because I hadn't finished my degree. But I soon realized that my skill set and drive were what truly mattered. With the grace of God and the support of mentors, I landed roles that I never imagined possible. I will always be thankful for David and for his encouragement that helped me flourish, build, and rebrand the company, and within a year, we secured several partnerships with pioneering brands in the blockchain space.

While my career in traditional industries provided a solid foundation, it was the discovery of blockchain and cryptocurrency that truly ignited my passion for innovation. My introduction to Web3 was not just a professional pivot, but a personal awakening—a realization that this technology had the power to transform lives, including my own.

Empowering Through Adversity: The Birth of Women of Basketball

Founding the Women of Basketball (WOB) NFT project has been one of the most rewarding experiences in the Web3 space. Despite the challenges, including difficulties with the initial platform we launched on, we persevered. We learned the importance of research and the value of making the process as easy as possible for consumers. Launching the Women of Basketball project was a pivotal moment in my career.

This project was born out of a desire to support and empower Junior College female basketball athletes who often face financial hardships and limited resources. The project provided a platform for these athletes to share their stories and bring awareness to their struggles. It was a challenging endeavor, especially in the early days when we encountered technical difficulties and had to pivot quickly to ensure the project's success. But through these challenges, I learned the importance of resilience, adaptability, and the power of community.

The WOB project was more than just a business venture; it was a mission to give voice to the voiceless and to shine a light on the inequities that exist in sports and beyond. As someone who has had to fight for every opportunity, I saw a reflection of my own journey in these athletes—women who were giving their all, yet often overlooked and underappreciated. The NFT space, with its emphasis on decentralization and empowerment, provided the perfect platform to elevate these stories and to create a movement around the need for greater support and recognition of female athletes.

Building the project was a labor of love, requiring me to take on roles I hadn't anticipated. Designing the artwork and collaborating with mentors like Mary Beth Sales and my daughter were crucial in bringing our vision to life. Their support and creativity helped shape the final product, and bringing "Women of Basketball" into fruition has been deeply rewarding.

These are the Women of Basketball NFT designs created with Leslie's direction to raise funds in support of Junior College athletes.

Opened Doors

WOB opened new doors for me, leading to opportunities I never could have imagined—such as speaking at the United Nations General Assembly Science Summit (UNGA78). Participating in this event was a profound experience, not just for me personally, but for the many women and girls who could see themselves in my story. It was a moment that underscored the importance of representation and the power of diverse voices in shaping the future of Web3.

At the UNGA78, I had the chance to discuss the intersection of blockchain technology, social impact, and the empowerment of women and underrepresented communities. It was an honor to be in a space where global leaders, innovators, and changemakers were gathered, all with a shared vision of using technology for good. This experience further solidified my belief in the potential of Web3 to drive meaningful change, not just in the digital realm, but in the lives of real people across the globe.

In the Web3 space, I connected with Sandy Martinez, who knew Cindy Coon and helped make it possible for many of us women to speak at the UN. The experience was surreal—I never imagined I would have the opportunity to speak at the United Nations. It was a significant milestone not only for me but for women of color everywhere, demonstrating that we can achieve whatever we set our minds to. It also serves to encourage young girls who look like me that anything is possible, and they too can accomplish their dreams.

This photo captures a moment with inspiring women from Women of Web3 that Leslie had the honor of speaking with at the United Nations 78th Science Summit in NYC 2023.

As I delved deeper into the Web3 space, the potential for impact became increasingly clear. Founding the Women of Basketball project was just the beginning. The connections I made and the lessons I learned during this time fueled my drive to explore even more ambitious ventures, both within and beyond the blockchain world.

Pioneering in Web3 My Role in Shaping the Future

My work with Gokhshtein Media has been both fulfilling and exciting. Through this platform, I have been able to amplify the voices of innovators, creators, and leaders in the blockchain space. Attending conferences like ETH Denver, NFT NYC, and Consensus has allowed me to stay at the forefront of industry developments and forge connections with some of the most brilliant minds in the Web3 space. From the concept of a water heater mining Bitcoin to advancements in digital asset computing, the projects we encounter are a testament to the boundless potential of blockchain technology.

Leslie during her speech at the United Nations 78th Science Summit in New York.

Collaborating with pioneers in the field has been both inspiring and exhilarating. The exposure to new ideas and the opportunity to contribute to the growth of the Web3 ecosystem continue to fuel my passion and drive. Creating inclusive environments within the Web3 community is not just about being welcoming—it's about actively dismantling barriers that have historically kept marginalized groups, particularly women, from thriving in technology and finance. I've learned through my journey that inclusion begins with listening. It's crucial to understand the unique challenges that women face in this space, from subtle biases to overt discrimination.

One of my strategies has been to create safe spaces where women can share their experiences without fear of judgment or dismissal. Whether through online communities, in-person events, or educational workshops, these spaces are designed to foster connection and mutual support. Women in Web3 need to see that they are not alone, that their voices matter, and that their contributions are invaluable to the future of this industry.

Another key aspect is representation. I believe that seeing women in leadership roles, as speakers at conferences, and as the faces of major projects is empowering. It sends a clear message that women belong here, and their presence is not just welcomed but essential. I've made it a point to advocate for women to be included on panels, in discussions, and in decision-making processes within Web3 companies and communities.

In addition to my work at Gokhshtein Media, I have also been involved in various initiatives aimed at fostering diversity and inclusion in the Web3 space. Whether it's mentoring young women who are just starting their careers in tech or collaborating with organizations that focus on providing resources and education to underrepresented communities, I am committed to using my platform to make a positive impact. The decentralized nature of Web3 offers a unique opportunity to create a more equitable digital landscape—one where individuals have control over their assets, their data, and their future.

Leslie speaking to youth about blockchain and financial literacy.
Photo Credit: Hizzyinc. Houston, TX.

Building Alliances

Building alliances has been one of the most rewarding aspects of my journey. In a space as rapidly evolving as Web3, collaboration is key. I've formed partnerships with organizations and individuals who share my commitment to gender equality and diversity in technology. These alliances have been instrumental in driving change and amplifying the voices of women in the industry.

One of my proudest moments was co-founding the Women of Basketball project. This initiative was not just about supporting female athletes; it was about creating a network of women who could rely on each other, share resources, and amplify each other's voices. Through this project, I've connected with other women-led initiatives in the Web3 space, creating a powerful network of support and collaboration.

These alliances extend beyond just women in Web3. I've worked with male allies who are committed to gender equality, recognizing that true inclusion requires the involvement of everyone. Together, we've launched campaigns, hosted events, and driven conversations that challenge the status quo and push for a more inclusive future in Web3.

Leslie with her Gokhshtein Media team participating at an event in Nashville, TN.

Community Building

Community building has been at the heart of my efforts to create a welcoming and supportive environment for women in Web3. I've always believed that a strong, inclusive community is essential for fostering innovation and growth. In this industry, where collaboration is key, it's vital that women feel they have a place where they belong and where their contributions are valued.

To build such a community, I've focused on creating spaces where women can connect, share their experiences, and support each other. This includes online forums, social media groups, and in-person events that bring women together. These communities are designed to be inclusive and supportive, where women can freely discuss their challenges, celebrate their successes, and collaborate on projects.

In addition to creating these spaces, I've worked to ensure that the community is continuously nurtured and grown. This involves organizing regular events, both online and offline, that keep the community engaged and provide opportunities for learning and networking. I've also encouraged community members to take on leadership roles within these spaces, helping to build a sense of ownership and responsibility for the community's growth.

Through these efforts, I've seen firsthand how powerful a strong community can be in empowering women. When women come together, they can achieve incredible things, and it's been my privilege to help facilitate that process.

Future of Web3

Looking ahead, I see a future where Web3 is not just a buzzword, but a fundamental part of our everyday lives. From finance and healthcare to education and entertainment, blockchain technology has the potential to revolutionize the way we live, work, and interact with one another. But for this future to become a reality, we must ensure that the benefits of Web3 are accessible to everyone, not just a select few. This means investing in education, advocating for inclusive policies, and creating platforms that empower individuals from all walks of life.

My focus remains on empowering women and underrepresented communities within the blockchain space. I am committed to exploring new projects and fields of interest, driven by a passion for creating meaningful change and advancing the Web3 ecosystem.

Through my work at Gokhshtein Media and my ongoing commitment to empowering underrepresented communities, I've had the privilege of contributing to the growth of the Web3 ecosystem. Yet, as I look back on all that has been achieved, I know that this is only the beginning. The path ahead is filled with endless possibilities, and I am eager to continue this journey of innovation and impact.

Conclusion

Reflecting on my journey from a small border town to the forefront of the Web3 world, my journey has been one of growth, resilience, and unwavering determination. As I continue to navigate this space, I am constantly reminded of the importance of staying true to my roots—of remembering where I came from and the values that have guided me throughout my life. Integrity, perseverance, and a commitment to lifting others up are at the core of everything I do, and I believe these principles are more important now than ever. The Web3 world is rapidly evolving, and as we move forward, we must ensure that we are building a future that is inclusive, equitable, and reflective of the diversity of our global community.

This is only the beginning, and I am excited to see where this path will lead. The road ahead is filled with challenges and opportunities, and I am ready to embrace them all, knowing that my journey can help pave the way for the next generation of innovators.

I am filled with gratitude for the experiences and opportunities that have shaped my path, and I hope that by sharing my story, I can inspire others—especially women and minorities—to pursue their dreams in the Web3 space.

As I bring this narrative to a close, I want to encourage you to reflect on your own journey. The stories and insights shared in this book are not just about my path; they are about the collective power of our experiences, our struggles, and our triumphs. Whether you are new to the Web3 space or a seasoned innovator, there is a place for you in this unfolding story.

Reflection

As you delve into the chapters of this book, I invite you to engage with the ideas and concepts presented here. Explore the resources provided, connect with the Web3 community, and consider how you, too, can contribute to this exciting and transformative space. The future of Web3 is being written now, and your voice is an essential part of that story.

The journey from higher education to the blockchain era is not just about technological advancement; it's about personal growth, societal change, and the relentless pursuit of a better, more inclusive world. As you embark on your own path in the Web3 world, remember that the challenges you face are opportunities in disguise, and the lessons you learn along the way will shape not just your future, but the future of this entire ecosystem. Let's build this future together, one block at a time.

Let's Connect

Leslie Motta
www.womenofweb3un.io/speakers/leslie-motta

CHAPTER FIVE

From Higher Education to the Blockchain Era: A Latina's Path in the Web3 World
By Sandy Martinez

I am the proud founder of Women of Web3 dedicated to being on a transformative journey to make a lasting social equality impact within the innovative digital ecosystem utilizing all my talents, skills, experience, and knowledge. My journey includes working with global brands and projects as a Web3 advisor and ambassador, becoming a radio host for my own Spanish Web3 radio show, my work being featured on Times Square twice within six months, and of course taking over 34 women to the United Nations Science Summit to share the power of blockchain technology and Web3. Talk about historical accomplishments from a former higher education leader turned Web3 strategist!

My success correlates directly with the diverse roles and experiences I've had throughout my life. My higher education career is certainly a big contributor, but I have always been a big dreamer. Having the vision of a dreamer has allowed me to create opportunities to make a difference in people's lives, just like my mentors and amazing leaders did for me. This support has defined my purpose and drive, and I feel honored to share my story with you—my roots, career, the unique experiences within Web3 as a Latina, and most importantly, why I want to encourage you to explore blockchain technology, Web3, and the digital asset industry. These technologies are transforming our world and understanding them is key to shaping a future where you thrive.

Roots and Wings

My roots have shaped me in so many ways. For decades, my father, grandfather and other relatives had migrated back and forth to the U.S. when workers were needed under the Bracero program and the like. My father, Ricardo Martinez, eventually wanted his family to be together, so when I was five, he brought us to the U.S. for a better life and a good education (Gracias Papi).

Left: Sandy's Father Ricardo Martinez De La Riva. Right: Sandy as a 5-year-old.

Life was far from easy as a low-income family living in Santa Ana, CA (why I love the Dodgers!). Then at age 14 my parents moved our family to Mesa, AZ. My parents struggled to pay their bills, to obtain good jobs with benefits or the opportunity of being promoted due to their limited educational background as both only made it to 1st and 2nd grade. They relied on free/reduced lunches, assistance from organizations like Chicanos Por La Causa and Christmas presents for us from the local fire department, which as a child, I thought was the coolest thing.

My parents were absent a lot from our household due to them having to work around the clock to provide for our family. I had no choice but to grow up and help fill in the gaps, help care for my siblings, assist with affairs that required translation, and basic accounting to help manage our household. Consequently, homework came last as these priorities were first. I had to self-motivate myself and prided myself on being a good student. I loved school and was excited to get good grades to show my parents, even though they didn't know what good grades signified.

What you see today is a product of public education and growing up before my time as the oldest of 5 in an immigrant household.

Through my upbringing, I learned how to overcome challenges, be a problem solver, and learned that higher education was a door that would provide me with the opportunities my parents never had. My father was my motivator and mentor who taught me the true meaning of having an extraordinary work ethic. I still remember him telling me in Spanish almost every morning as he drank his Folgers coffee, "Always be on time, Sandra. Be a good-mannered employee and pay attention." I am proud to share my story with you today as an immigrant from Piedra Gorda in Zacatecas, Mexico as a first-generation non-traditional college student that broke glass ceilings as a higher education professional and leader at Arizona State University (ASU) for almost two decades. You can certainly say, I am living the dream my parents dreamed for me.

My upbringing has shaped me into a passionate advocate for education, a dedicated community builder, a champion for Hispanic and Latino voices, and an inspiring motivational speaker. I am the Founder and CEO of Strive Studio Career Coaching & Consulting to support women of color to thrive in their careers and assist organizations in my areas of expertise such as diversity, equity and inclusion, organizational culture, Web3 advising, and staff success initiatives.

I am also passionate about empowering women serving as an engaged Board Member of Young & Empowered Women's Association and United Latinas elevating women across the nation and beyond providing mentorship and guidance. It's a beautiful thing to be amongst mentees and professionals that share similar backgrounds, dreams, and roots. I am so grateful these communities exist.

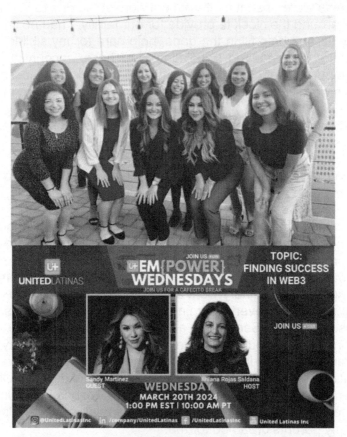

Top: Young and Empowered Women Networking Event, October 2021. Bottom: Sandy speaking to United Latinas about Web3 with Co-President and Mentor, Ilhiana Rojas Saldana

The Digital Leap – Education and Early Career

Technology has always fascinated me. I remember the first time I used a computer; I was in junior high, and I was hooked! Since then, I have always been intrigued by how things worked. I was delighted when my cousin Victor Noriega and family got their first computer because that was the first time I learned about AOL and heard "You've Got Mail." I quickly learned how to join chats and look up information. In school, I signed up for computer classes and did my best to be a good typist. I wanted to be savvy with all thing's computers! I knew that would be key to my success in getting a good job to help my family. When I got my first computer, I was thrilled to own a piece of technology that could expand my knowledge and change my life.

During my undergrad studies, I took more technology classes learning HTML coding and how to design websites. I also learned how to navigate the complex intricacies of Excel, which helped me considerably in my university roles. Before I knew it, I was using the AutoHotKey application to streamline my work. A coworker taught me how to program it to automatically send emails from an Excel sheet to Outlook and then document the details in the comments of each student account on PeopleSoft. It amazed me how this command did all the work and all I had to do was watch technology take over my job with minimal to no interference on my end. I felt like an innovator, haha! I happily taught other peers how to do it too and loved that feeling of helping them be efficient like me.

I then took more technology courses in graduate school and landed a graduate practicum with the ASU's Center for Gender Equity in Science and Technology. I was inspired by how they had culturally responsive education programs that taught high school girls how to program robots by having them present solutions for issues that existed within their communities as well as how to strengthen their storytelling skills with software programs. I remember one instance vividly where a Latina high school student doing her final presentation was looking at me for validation that she was doing a good job. I knew then that I wanted to do more for girls to learn about Science, Technology, Engineering and Math (STEM), especially for girls of color like me because it truly matters when people that look like you are in the room.

Balancing a Career and University Commitments

If you ask anyone that knows me, they will tell you that I am a proud Sun Devil.

I lived and breathed ASU 24/7. Not only did I have a transformative career at ASU, which I will share next, but I hold a Bachelor of Arts in Human Communication, a minor in Business, and a Master's in Higher and Postsecondary Education with a focus on university administration both obtained while working full-time, raising my two sons, Christopher Andrew and Marco Jair, and as an engaged student and employee.

As a student, I was very involved since my day role did not have opportunities to advance. I was a student leader with the Association of Human Communication (AHC) taking on roles like Treasurer and

Vice President to help me get experience in event planning, becoming a public speaker, and university operations such as appropriations and budgets. I met incredible peers who I am still connected to.

Sandy's first public speaking roles with AHC during her undergraduate years. Left: The first AHC Career Fair. Right: Opening remarks for the HopeLine Domestic Violence Campaign at ASU sponsored by Verizon Wireless.

During this time, I also met Dr. Angela Trethewey who not only was my professor, but the assistant director of my program who talked me out of quitting during my bachelors. You see, I felt guilty that I was a mom (and a wife back then) spending most of my time at the university either working or in school. I'll never forget when she shared her story and reminded me that it would never be a bad example showing my kids the value I placed on education, plus you never know what life would throw at you, so we always need to depend on ourselves. That left a lasting impact on me, and I never felt guilty pursuing my studies again.

My key accomplishments as a student leader were organizing outstanding networking and career exploration events and working collaboratively with businesses and university departments to develop opportunities to help enhance ASU students' experiences. I also had secured my first ever sponsorship with Verizon Wireless to hold a campus-wide drive to provide domestic violence victims with phones and resources. Lastly, I was very hands on as Vice President of AHC to rebrand the organization, so this was my first experience building a brand and handling all strategic communication and marketing.

After my bachelors, all this service paid off since I was able to share this tangible evidence of my leadership skills, talents, dedication to support students, and as a community architect.

Top: Sandy celebrating her master's degree with friend Diana Aguirre Rosales (Right Cap). Grad cap message is dedicated to her cousin Claudia Martinez who lost her battle with Cancer. Bottom: Sandy with her grandmother, Maria De Jesus Noriega after her bachelor's ceremony.

My professional trajectory is interesting. My first job was as a receptionist at Queen of Peace Parish, my local parish since I grew up in a strict Catholic family that attended mass every Sunday. I had volunteered for years as an usher during mass, so when the opportunity came up, it was perfect. I then worked for a bank as an Account Manager managing credit cards, gaining valuable insights in loss prevention that made me a good negotiator with a strong set of customer service skills. This role was a huge reason I transitioned to work at ASU and moved up within two months. Getting the ASU job was not easy though as I had no resume and did not have good interviewing skills. My good friend Rosie Garcia, however, saw my potential so much that she invested time in showing me how to put a resume together. By the time we were done, I was amazed at how brilliantly she articulated my skills and experience. I was a rockstar and I didn't even know it, ha-ha. Without Rosie, I would not have started my career at ASU. She truly inspired my passion for career coaching.

My higher education career at ASU began as an Account Specialist in the Student Business Services loss prevention area managing university accounts and providing financial counseling to students. I later managed the fiscal, human resources, and daily operations in the School of Transborder Studies. My journey also included working at the College of Health Solutions Dean's Office first in business operations and later as the Manager of Administrative Support Operations and Staff Success where I was responsible for the college's employee engagement and improvement programs, professional development budget, onboarding initiatives, staff internal communications, and managing the college's administrative operations on the executive and academic levels with a team close to 15 professional staff and 5 student employees.

My last role at ASU was as the Director for the Center for Gender Equity in Science and Technology leading the center's operations and fiscal affairs. Yes, I became the Director of that same center that I did my graduate practicum in that inspired me to work in STEM. During this time, I heard about crypto currencies and non-fungible tokens (NFT's) or digital assets since a global business leader I had met on LinkedIn was now part of the team for the first crypto hotel that was planned to hit the Phoenix market. I knew very little, but I realized that it was important for me to educate myself and students about this fascinating emerging technology.

Luckily, my friend introduced me to the CEO of EV Hotel and long story short I was brave enough to reach out. It wasn't long before I arranged for him and his executive team to visit ASU to talk to our tourism students and fellow university administrators. Shortly after that, my time at ASU ended (this calls for another book), and I purchased my first NFT on my last day at ASU. That's how I entered Web3 and began an adventure of a lifetime, which is the journey I'm taking you with me in what follows, but first I want to share a little more about my ASU experience and insights on leadership as a Latina higher education professional.

I have always enjoyed being of service in my community. At ASU, I was highly embedded. I had the honor and privilege to have served as the Chicano Latino Faculty and Staff Association's (CLFSA) 50th President where I had contributed as a member, mentor and as the Student Liaison managing the Laura I. Rendon Scholarship program for over 8 years. I was also a proud member of the ASU Commission on the Status of Women (CSW) for over a decade supporting professional development and mentoring opportunities for our university community. This led me to be CSW chair for the Tempe Campus twice.

Pictures from the ASU Chicano Latino Faculty and Staff Associations 50th Anniversary Gala that Sandy Executively produced as President of the organization. Bottom: Pictures with Provost Mark Searle, Co-host, Journalist and Faculty Vanessa Ruiz, and the now first ASU Latina Provost, Nancy Gonzales (on the right).

Sandy, as CLFSA president, reading the Very Hungry Caterpillar by
Eric Carle to pre-school students for the CLFSA Holiday Drive.

Looking back, I am happy knowing I created programs that are still standing today like the CLFSA Cultivating Latin Líderes events to help faculty and staff thrive in their ASU careers, which my son Christopher helped me create the title for. Being of service to students was the most rewarding. Watching them graduate always left me with tears of joy. As a result of all my contributions, I was honored to have been recognized as a Badass Women of ASU.

I am very proud of the heights I reached at ASU, both as a student and as an employee. The path to leadership was not an easy one. One of the biggest motivators for me to get my bachelor's and master's degree in higher and postsecondary education at the time was the fact that there are very few Chicano Latino faculty and staff nationwide in this field. In the book Latino Educational Leadership: Serving Latino Communities and Preparing Latinx Leaders Across the P-20 Pipeline by Rodriguez, Martinez, and Valle (2018), I learned there was only 5% of full-time college administrators who are Latinos/as and the majority of those were in positions of moderate to low prestige. Knowing this motivated me to become the most effective Latina university administrator I could be, striving to create opportunities for faculty, staff, and students of color.

It is a difficult and lonely journey at times being a first-generation student and higher education professional of color because many cannot relate to you. We are often the "firsts" in our families to achieve these goals. Overall, having representation for people like me is crucial to the success of Latino/a faculty, staff, and campus leaders. Representing people of color can have a lasting positive impact in the retention of Latino/a college students, especially when those students can relate to you, they see themselves in you, you inspire them, and you get to create a sense of belonging.

Now, there were many challenges and barriers to overcome too, but with each setback I became stronger, and it pushed me to keep working harder to advance my career. I can honestly say that my success was the result of the below things:

- Dreaming big, but intentionally (I'll share more at the end)
- Building genuine relationships along the way
- Making time for self-care and a good workout at CrossFit Incite
- Taking advantage of professional development opportunities
- Investing in my education with the tuition waiver ASU offered
- Going to mass or doing anything that strengthened my faith to be a good leader

I was very strategic in where and how I invested my time. Your network is also key. I was fortunate to have CLFSA and CSW to help me navigate my academic journey and higher education career. I wouldn't be where I am today without my CLFSA & CSW "familia" because through these organizations I gained mentors, colleagues who have become friends, and valuable opportunities to help me grow professionally and personally.

ASU Hispanic Convocation 2019.

Top: Celebrating Ulises Estrada's bachelors' graduation with School of Transborder Studies Staff. Bottom Left: At mentee Diana Quintero's Masters Graduation. Bottom Right: Grad invite for mentee Rosalia Hernandez-Gonzalez.

I will always treasure the students, faculty and staff I mentored. Watching them succeed, and sometimes make more money than me was very rewarding. I know how it feels to be the first in our families' navigating things on our own and quite often having to feel the pressure of juggling multiple responsibilities. I know how it is being a person of color and not be understood or even seen for the hard work we do. All my mentees, however, always inspired me more than they could ever know. They truly were the fuel that kept me going.

My most memorable time will be sharing this journey with my sons, especially since they motivated me in so many ways like pushing me to redo my personal statement for grad school and taking more than one class when I started. They were my favorite office guests who got to experience college life with me and meet amazing humans like America Ferrera at a young age. Most importantly, they made it to a university, they made it to ASU too!

Left: Sandy's son Marco helping carry her books near Hayden Library, Tempe Campus. Middle: Sandy's sons after a lunch with her at ASU Downtown Campus. Right: Hugs after Christopher graduated from ASU.

Throughout my university life, I have had many people who took the time to be there for me, to give me advice, to support my goals, and dreams. I am so grateful for them. I am also very grateful for my family, especially my grandma who always prayed I got good grades and my siblings who helped me juggle things for my sons (love you, Diane, Manny, Jr, and Erik). I will forever be thankful to my mentors Dr. Gabriel Escontrias Jr. and Dr. Lisa Magaña who would be available in seconds whenever I needed them. Karen Engler also has a special place in my heart for seeing the leader in me always welcoming me, my thoughts and ideas as we built professional development programs for university staff and faculty.

All of them knew the bigger picture of why people like me should lead in settings like these. This is why I am passionate about diversity and inclusion in the workplace, giving back by connecting others to opportunities, and why I coach and mentor others with their career and educational goals. I feel very privileged to have a strong background as a higher education professional and leader. I admire those that came before me to pave the way. Because of this, I am a lifelong learner committed to using my privilege for good while being a voice for my community, always striving to lead by example and honoring my parents, Ricardo and Blanca, in everything I do.

The Web 3 Awakening

The first Web3 project I was part of with an NFT was for a metavestor club for global business leaders. I got into the project because of my work with the executives from the crypto Hotel as I was given a Whitelist (WL) or VIP pass to be able to enter the project by having an opportunity to purchase the NFT before it went public. When I was asked for my MetaMask (digital wallet), my Twitter and my Discord ID I felt like this was a foreign language. I had to Google what a WL and Discord was and immediately started my Twitter account. I had to ask tons of questions to my friend Curtis Cecil who I knew had crypto.

Entering the Web3 ecosystem was a significant challenge for me, even as a tech-savvy Latina, which made me realize how difficult it must be for others. I quickly identified that the major barriers were education, language, and technology. Determined to make a difference, I committed myself to learning everything I could so that I could help others navigate this complex space. I began building friendships with people from around the world, many of whom were learning alongside me. I realized that women and Spanish-speaking investors needed extra support, not just in understanding their investments but also in staying informed.

To bridge this gap, I co-hosted Twitter Spaces (now X Spaces) in Spanish, translating vital information and updates so our community could make informed decisions and expand their networks. This hands-on involvement allowed me to fully immerse myself in the digital landscape, where I connected with top influencers in Web3 and began sharing my expertise as a Latina professional and career coach. Through this journey, I established myself as a leader within the Hispanic Web3 community, helping to empower others and contribute to their growth.

This investment in Web3 led to the most unexpected and rewarding experiences. At the Young & Empowered Annual Conference in 2022, I had the chance to participate in the mentoring segment, where I proudly talked about the work I was doing in the Web3 space. During one of the mentoring circles, I had a brief but impactful conversation with Laura Madrid, the trailblazing Latina who owns La Onda 1190 AM, the first Latina-owned radio station in Arizona. Intrigued by her story, I followed up with Laura the following week, eager to learn more about her journey. Little did I know our lunch meeting would lead to an extraordinary opportunity—Laura was so captivated by my story that she offered me the chance to host my own radio show about Web3!

Naturally, my imposter syndrome kicked in, and I immediately told her that I couldn't possibly do it alone—I needed a co-host, maybe someone from the Forbes top 10 Latinos in Web3. But Laura wasn't having it. She insisted that I had everything I needed to lead this on my own. And just like that, I walked away from our lunch meeting with my own radio show! Now, picture me sitting in my car, on the phone with my dear friend Lupe, crying tears of joy as I shared this incredible news. Fast forward a few weeks, and there I was again, sitting in the car, tears streaming down my face as I heard my radio show promo for the first time. It was a surreal moment, one that reminded me of just how far I've come.

Sandy's first radio show announcement for Webtr3s Al Aire.

This unbelievable opportunity pushed me to become the dynamic WebTr3s al Aire radio show host dedicated to informing and educating the Spanish speaking community about the Web3 and NFT industry to ensure our community does not stay behind. The programming included an education and news segment with a special guest that was a trailblazer in the industry. As an education advocate and experienced higher education leader, I believe in education as a powerful tool to empower others, so having my own radio show to do just that was a dream, but I was ready for it and Laura knew it. Her believing in me was the powerful push I needed.

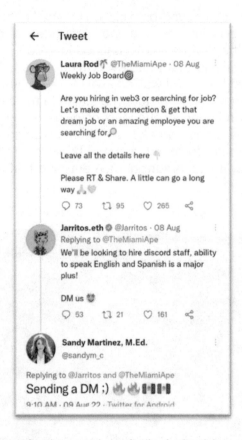

Twitter post Sandy responded to for the Jarritos job opportunity.

A month later, I came across a Twitter post by The Miami Ape, a Web3 Latina leader and influencer, where Jarritos shared that they were looking for staff for their Discord. I never thought that responding with fire emojis and Mexican flags would lead me to work for a global brand that has so much sentimental value to me and my family as a Mexican. Shortly after that response, I sent a DM or direct message to Jarritos and connected with their Web3 Director and expressed that not only I could help them manage their Discord, but with my educational and professional background I could contribute way more to the success of the project, including helping them cultivate a community in Web3 with my established networks and support the launch of their first NFT collection. That's how I created my own position and became the Jarritos Web3 Ambassador. It was surreal that I got to work for a family-owned company that has elevated Mexican culture for decades globally since 1950.

You are probably wondering why Jarritos entered Web3. Well, Jarritos entered this new industry with the Bones NFT Collection with the purpose to build community while disrupting the industry and educating and onboarding new users from all walks of life from anywhere around the world while bringing good values in addition to expressing my beautiful Mexican culture.

Sandy's digital identity or PFP on Twitter was this Bones by Jarritos NFT when she served as the brands Web3 Ambassador. Sandy still owns this NFT.

The collection was very meaningful with special artwork. First, because it uses skeletons and cultural relevance. I mean we all have wesitos or bones. Anyone can identify regardless of gender, race, ethnicity, color, or creed. We can dress them up and put them in real life situations relevant to all cultures worldwide, which fulfills the purpose as a brand that celebrates diversity and being inclusive to all people. Second, the NFT art is beautiful. It was created by two talented and brilliant female Mexican Artists, Perla Perez and Rocio Thomas with the direction of Severino Alvarez Truely, Jarritos's creative director at the time. The wesitos are decorated with our favorite traits celebrating Mexican culture, fashion worldwide, lifestyle, and Web3. All of this was a source of pride for me as an immigrant who spent hours on our vacations with my grandfather, Vicente

Noriega or Papa Chente at his little store in Zacatecas, Mexico drinking Jarritos (go team Mandarin!).

Miami Art Week 2022 pictures from the Jarritos event with holders (middle) and Eric Delamare, Jarritos CMO (right)

Through my work with Jarritos, I had various exciting responsibilities. I helped launch the NFT project (not really sleeping for a month during this phase), represented the brand on virtual and at Web3, blockchain, and art related events and conferences. I remember going to Mexico City as a guest speaker with Hola Metaverso for their Leaders and Builders in Web3 event to find a room filled with people very proud that Jarritos was part of Web3. I was pleasantly surprised that some leaders and guests even traveled from different parts of Mexico just to meet me and express their joy for the brand's move. I also got to meet with holders and connect with the robust Mexican Web3 community making lifelong friends.

One of my most favorite parts in this role was also to bring our community together through our X Spaces. I served as host and created educational programming often elevating our culture and building community by creating spaces to recognize Hispanic and Latino leaders in Web3. I had the honor to work with Fox Deportes, Los Charros de Jalisco, Cuban American Country artist Sammy Arriaga, Web3 creatives, and prominent Web3 projects like the Bored Ape Yacht Club, and Space Riders to name a few.

My Web3 growth didn't end there. I continued expanding my network, meeting some incredible women. Some of them, like my friend and talented illustrator Lucia Diaz, launched digital collections to give back to orphanages in Colombia, others like Leslie Motta joined media companies and are now running operations. I had seen how illustrators and designers had built their brands, and how they had extended opportunities to educate and onboard others to Web3, so they too could build in the space.

Jarritos Twitter Space Announcement with Fox Deportes that Sandy hosted for Hispanic Heritage Month 2022.

Seeing this technology being used for good left me very inspired and that's when I first had it in my heart to speak on global platforms like the United Nations (UN) either with my own social impact project one day or to share the stories of the women paving the way in this industry.

Then in December 2022, I got a call from my former ASU Executive Coach, Cyndi Coon, yes also an author here, to catch up. I shared all the incredible work that I was doing, only to end the call with tears because I was asked what I wanted to accomplish the following year, and I said to speak at the UN to share the power of blockchain technology. Well, she responded, "Done." I had no idea that my former coach and close friend Cyndi also worked with the UN helping organize the Science Summit each year. I remember immediately calling my friend Lucia Diaz right after to share that WE were going to the UN. We both cried. This is when the work began to launch Women of Web3.

Spring 2023 was incredibly rewarding. We started working on the session proposal and programming for the UN's 78th Science Summit, and when Cyndi mentioned the challenge of finding 17 women speakers, I already had a list of amazing women I'd met in Web3. Every woman I invited was moved to tears, selected for their contributions and support within the ecosystem. As the session approached, I was grateful for the overwhelming support, especially from Debora Carrizo and her team in Argentina, who created our website and graphics pro bono. I also learned ChatGPT and Canva to create our marketing campaign. With Lucia Diaz's help, we secured The Canvas 3.0, in collaboration with WHIM as our venue that was perfect for bridging the digital and physical realms in Web3. More great partners joined, making the event truly special.

Left: Group picture after Sandy participated in the Latinas in Web3 panel for NFTNYC 2023. Right: Sandy with Marisa Estrada at the University of Medellin speaking on building community through technology.

As our UN session in New York approached, a series of incredible opportunities unfolded. I traveled to Colombia to speak at the University of Medellin, thanks to my Hola Metaverso family.

We collaborated with Bueno and Neefter to launch the first-ever NFT for Women of Web3, led by our talented artist Anana and digital asset liaison Mauricio (also authors in this book), to raise funds for STEM scholarships and support NFT artists and Metaverse developers.

Together with Illustrator and Women of Web3 speaker Lucia Diaz, a proud first-generation Colombian, we also organized an art exhibit that honored over 100+ Latin American artists and individuals with

Latin American roots in the U.S. Additionally, Sandy Carter, another featured speaker, and I were interviewed for an International World Peace Day segment in Europe. We also began planning international Sustainable Development Goals (SDG) panels for the When Worlds Collide event by Let's Disrupt Digital and wrapped it all up with a photoshoot for our women and a beautiful brunch, thanks to the Chopra Foundation.

What began as a one-time UN initiative to spotlight female trailblazers in the digital landscape has evolved into Women of Web3, an organization with unforgettable moments and a meaningful mission. We created the first NFT tied to a UN session and made history with our UNGA78 session, "Women in the Web3 Space: Reducing Inequalities Through Digital and Technological Opportunities," the first all-women Web3 and blockchain panel at the UN, with 70% Latina representation. This led to our NFT funding scholarships with Mexican startup Epic Queen, helping young girls learn about AI and earn Blockchain Analyst Certificates. Seeing the scholarship recipients have access to these opportunities reaffirmed our commitment to empowering more women in the digital space.

Opening remarks for the Women of Web3 Session for the United Nations 78th Science Summit in NYC with Ana Isabel Rivas Fernandez (Left) and Cyndi Coon to Sandy's Right.

With Women of Web3, we have traveled together for speaking engagements from New York to Miami and other notable places. We have been a source of inspiration and motivation for each other when that imposter syndrome kicks in as we grow. We have opened doors for each other allowing us to partake in exclusive opportunities. Every bit of hard work has been worth it, and I would do it all over again because it is sweet to see your brilliant and intelligent friends thrive.

My Web3 journey has led to other unique opportunities and recognition. I was a Co-MC for the boy band Menudo in their Latin Music Showcase in Miami March 2023 thanks to my friend Alyssa Wolfe from FanMax. I had been a fan of the original group, so I was thrilled they had a new group of talented young men continue the brand, especially in Web3 with their NFT project. This was a night to remember as my friend Sammy Arriaga, who was also a Web3 featured artist, sang my favorite songs.

I also volunteered my time as Director of International Communications for Maya Spirits who has been recognized as the most impactful Web3 social impact project in Mexico. This remarkable Web3 Charitable Organization uses blockchain technology and the essence of transformative art to support the Mexican indigenous community in the Calakmul jungle to directly empower them with education, technology, resources to become entrepreneurs and so much more.

I have had the honor of being featured in Times Square for NFT NYC and for my work with Women of Web3 in 2023. I was also recognized as a 100 Most Inspirational Women of Web3 & AI for 2023 by Unstoppable Women of Web3. It has also been rewarding to grow as a speaker being interviewed by platforms like TIMEPieces (TIME Magazine's Web3 Community) and Gokhshtein Media and speaking at NFTNYC, NFTLA events, and at the University of Medellin just prior to the UN. I had the privilege to attend exclusive events with prominent projects and Web3 organizations like Pudgy Penguins, Rug Radio, and more of course bringing my Women of Web3 speakers with me. Lastly, I have created opportunities for women to be visible by speaking their name when opportunities came up and hosting events to bring communities together like a Vision Board event with Mujeres of all Shades in Arizona that empowers women to feel their best on and off the runway as well as sessions like "Fashion, Innovation & Impact" featuring fashion powerhouses at NFTNYC events with our partners from Let's Disrupt Digital and Bitbasel.

Sandy at NFT NYC 2024 events with Women of Web3 members.

During my Web3 journey, I faced numerous challenges that tested my resilience and commitment to making a lasting impact. Despite my best efforts and formal agreements, there were times I took on roles without receiving the promised compensation or benefit. This experience of working without pay was compounded by having to tolerate unprofessional behavior and microaggressions from some in the industry.

Building my brand and establishing my name required significant investment, both in terms of time and resources. It was a daunting task, but I constantly reminded myself of the bigger picture: ensuring that our communities do not fall behind, as we often have in other industries. I understood that my journey was not just about my personal success; it was about representing those who look like me and paving the way for others, especially women. This helped me move forward with a positive perspective.

I am grateful for everyone who has supported my growth, prayed with me or even covered my lodging to attend conferences when times were tough. All of this left the mark on me that together we can create meaningful change, demonstrating that diversity truly matters, and that community is at the heart of it all.

Current Ventures

Currently, I am fully immersed in building a solid foundation for Women of Web3. I am also proudly leading efforts to feature a new cohort at the UN Science Summits, while also making this book a reality. My focus extends to collaborating with organizations that share our mission to elevate and empower female leaders, creators, and developers in fostering gender equality within the Web3 and digital assets sectors in alignment with the United Nations Sustainable Development Goals 5 and 10, reduced inequalities and gender equality. I'm also very passionate about creating job opportunities for our featured speakers, driving me to continue this essential work with partners and leaders in the field. Through WW3, it's exciting work to elevate women, build community, create projects to raise money for scholarships for STEM education, and establish revenue streams to support our important and impactful work.

I'm also deeply committed to growing Strive Studio Career Coaching and Consulting, as I see a strong need for tailored support to help women of color advance in their careers. Additionally, I'm excited to expand my reach as a motivational speaker, sharing my powerful story to inspire others. Lastly, as a bilingual Web3 Advisor and Strategist with deep knowledge of the Hispanic and Latino markets, I'm uniquely positioned to educate and onboard communities, helping them understand and embrace blockchain technology, crypto, and the transformative potential of Web3. I'm passionate about meeting the specific needs of these communities and am thrilled to collaborate with organizations eager to implement this technology and make a lasting impact in the digital landscape.

Overall, I am staying open to learning more about this digital landscape. This journey is ever evolving, and I am excited to work with other thinkers and pioneers in the field to create meaningful change, so I am open to different opportunities. I'm thrilled to work with organizations that use blockchain technology for good. In this field, where no one is yet an expert, we have the unique opportunity to build and grow together.

Looking Ahead

As we've expressed throughout this book, blockchain technology holds immense power and potential. The Web3 and digital asset industry is revolutionary, offering innovative solutions that will impact our daily lives. NFTs are no longer just digital art; they provide opportunities like fractionalized ownership, wealth distribution, exclusive experiences, and represent real-world objects such as art, music, game items, videos, and even homes. We will see more brands entering Web3 to create immersive experiences for us as consumers, at times through a metaverse or cyberspace, where humans can interact socially and economically as digital figures. We must be ready for that!

Keith Grossman, President of Moonpay (and former President of TIME Magazine), coined the term "Warm Crypto" to describe projects and initiatives that use tech and respective Web3 communities for "good" – furthering tech literacy, education, outreach, and accessibility. This term perfectly encapsulates one of my favorite aspects of this technology. Using Warm Crypto to benefit society and being the good stewards the industry needs excites me more than I can express. It's deeply tied to my "why" – making a difference in someone's life.

In summary, I envision myself advancing in this industry, utilizing my God-given talents to build bridges and make a difference through Women of Web3. This technology is here to stay, and it will transform the way we live our daily lives. Furthermore, I firmly believe that good people always find good people to do good, so I look forward to collaborating with innovative thinkers who want to change the world, create access to education, and empower our communities.

Conclusion

Reflecting on this extraordinary journey through the Web3 space, I am filled with immense gratitude and pride for the milestones achieved and the road still ahead. Empowering my Hispanic and Latino community, creating opportunities for women, and educating others about this transformative industry have been central to my mission. This path has taken me to unimaginable heights—traveling more than ever before, realizing my dream of speaking at the UN, and even hosting my own radio show to share insights with a global audience.

I've had the privilege of becoming an international speaker at pivotal events shaping our digital future and being part of a historic moment with Jarritos. Having the President of Pudgy Penguins support Women of Web3 through our NFT was incredibly special. Witnessing my dear friend Marisa (Ritzy) Estrada, an extraordinary member of Women of Web3 and fellow Mexicana, take the stage at VeeCon 2024, meeting Gary Vee, and sharing memorable moments with Jay Shetty are powerful experiences I will treasure forever.

My story is a testament to the power of dreams, determination to reinvent myself, and community. I hope it inspires upcoming innovators in the Web3 space to pursue their passions relentlessly, knowing that they too can achieve greatness and create a lasting impact. The journey continues, and with it, the endless possibilities of what we can accomplish together in the world of Web3. Lastly, my heart is also full seeing the sisterhood being created with WW3 that elevates us beyond our imagination. Our initiatives wouldn't have accomplished so much without those choosing to amplify our voices and our work. I am deeply thankful to all those acknowledged in this book.

Reflection

As I write this chapter, I reflect on how challenging my life journey has been. I come from a small ranchito or town in Zacatecas, Mexico, where my parents' home is still unfinished—a constant reminder of how far I've come and how grateful I am for the life I get to live.

Martinez Family home back in Zacatecas Mexico, 2023

In high school, many doubted I would graduate because I was a single mom. But I did it proudly anyway. During the end of grad school, I was going through one of the lowest points in my life, but I graduated on time thanks to my friend Lupe Espinosa and Patricia Corona who supported me. These experiences, though tough, have shaped me into the determined trailblazer I am today. They remind me that I am worthy of success, regardless of the challenges I face and/or when other people don't believe in me. My tribe and purpose have truly guided me towards making my dreams a reality.

So, to anyone seeking success in their career and life, I offer this advice:

1. **Be Embedded in Your Organization and Community.** Leverage all available resources and get deeply involved in your organization or community because your contributions matter. Invest your time in activities or committees, and volunteer to share your talents and expertise. By actively adding value and being of service, you'll build a strong reputation while preparing for future opportunities and ensuring others recognize and appreciate your strengths and contributions.

2. **Build Genuine Relationships.** The genuine relationships I've built have led to invaluable mentorships and guidance, and this continues in Web3. My network has opened doors to job opportunities and exciting projects, enabling me to connect with people and support meaningful causes.

3. **Dream BIG Intentionally.** Ask yourself: Who is your future self? What do you want to accomplish? What role do you envision for yourself? What do you want your life to look like? Invest time in working towards that. Make decisions today that your future self will appreciate. As Benjamin Hardy states in his book *Personality Isn't Permanent*, "It's your responsibility to set your future self up for as much opportunity, success, and joy as possible. This is how you become the person and create the life you want, rather than becoming someone with regret."

4. **Don't be Afraid to Walk Away**. Jen Gottlieb, in her book *Be Seen*, wisely states, "When you say no to something that doesn't serve you, you're saying yes to growth, and development, and above all, yourself." It's crucial to feel valued in an organization, especially as immigrants and people of color, where our diverse perspectives and resourcefulness are our strengths. We should be respected for our contributions and whole selves. If not, it's okay to move on.

5. **Think This Too Shall Pass.** Remember, there will be hard times—but they are temporary, and each season has its purpose. As a leader, I've leaned on faith and kept Jeremiah 29:11 close: "For I know the plans I have for you, plans to prosper you and not to harm you, plans to give you hope and

a future." This verse has been my anchor during moments of difficulty and uncertainty. Faith taught me to trust God, even in unanswered prayers, knowing He has a greater plan. So, no matter the season you are in—whether joyful or difficult—trust Him. Lead with faith and know that hardships are lessons that strengthen and prepare you for the path ahead.

As my chapter concludes, I hope you've enjoyed this glimpse into my journey from higher education to the blockchain era. Witnessing the growth of women in Web3 has been a privilege, and it's clear that together, we can achieve far more than alone. With only 25% of tech jobs held by women globally (World Economic Forum, 2021), there's still much work to be done and I hope you join me. Be an agent of change by supporting WW3, hiring the incredible women featured here, and joining us in empowering women in emerging technology to build a legacy of success and innovation globally. In a world where barriers exist, let us be the bridges that connect dreams to reality

Let's Connect

Sandy Martinez
www.womenofweb3un.io/speakers/sandra-martinez
linktr.ee/sandy.martinez

CHAPTER SIX

The Art of Self-Embrace:
Blooming in The Unlikeliest of Places
By Wildy Martinez

With a luggage full of art supplies, I made my way through the very familiar streets of Herald Square in New York City, about to have one of my biggest dreams come true. Just four years prior, I was working as a Design Director for an activewear brand, overseeing the womenswear team just down the street on 5th Avenue. My office had a view of the Empire State Building, and I was at the pinnacle of my professional career as a fashion designer. Like many of us, I was oblivious to the fact that we were headed into a global pandemic that would lead to my entire division being shut down and losing my job.

Fast forward to May 2, 2024, I entered Macy's on 34th Street, mesmerized by the beautiful flowers—so many flowers.

It was their annual Macy's Flower Show, and I remembered my parents bringing my siblings and me to see the flowers and displays when we were kids. As I made my way through the lobby, I saw the

'Dior' sign and headed up the stairs, where I was warmly welcomed by the Miss Dior team.

Live sketching at Macy's Herald Square for Dior.

"Are you Wildy? We are so excited to have you as our live artist for Miss Dior." It was a "someone pinch me" moment. I could not believe this was happening, and I was filled with gratitude, knowing that the Web3 ecosystem had led me to this moment in my artistic career. Two years of exploring fashion and art with emerging technologies such as artificial intelligence, blockchain, and Web3 had given me opportunities I could never have imagined. I became an internationally featured artist, an AI Fashion Week finalist, and saw my art displayed on walls, wine bottles, coffee, and now Dior. It was, and still is, so surreal, especially because in 2021, my small family and I decided to move out of New York City to North Carolina. I questioned myself so many times if that was the right move for me professionally.

Looking back, though I enjoyed my job, I used it as a safety net to keep me from exploring the urge in me to start something of my own. It was timely that the moment I decided to step into the "new" and embrace my gifts was the moment I got furloughed again, this time from my remote job. It was as if I was cornered into looking inside and being reminded that I needed to push through the fear of starting something not just new, but for myself. There is a quote by Mel Robbins that changed everything for me in this transitional season of my life: "You need to hear this loud and clear: No one is coming. It is up to you. It has always been and will always be up to you."

I knew from a young age that I wanted to be an entrepreneur, and I was born to be an artist of some kind, especially since my love for fashion began when I was just six years old. Sometimes, it is necessary for doors to close, for rejections to happen, and for expectations to go unmet because it is in these moments that you are met with the most pivotal person you will ever meet—yourself.

In 2022, I entered the world of Web3, NFTs, and the crypto community. A year later, I was back in New York, showcasing my work in two galleries, Times Square, the New York Chamber of Commerce, and NFT NYC, one of the biggest NFT events in the world. The year after that, I was honored to be one of the speakers at the United Nations 78th Science Summit, discussing the evolution of art and fashion in AI and blockchain.

This is my story, a testament to the idea that it is never too late to rediscover your passions and pursue your dreams. Stepping into the unknown can lead to unimaginable opportunities and personal growth.

Roots and Wings

Growing up in the lively and diverse community of Washington Heights, New York City, my childhood was a vibrant tapestry woven with the rich sounds, colors, and traditions of Dominican culture. I am a first-generation Dominican American; my grandparents on my father's side immigrated to New York City in the 70s. My dad came later in 1977, after all his siblings, and shortly after, he was able to bring my mom, as they were already married by then. By the 1980s, our apartment building was a multigenerational household. Imagine growing up with uncles, aunts, and cousins either in the same building or on the same street. This closeness to family was the cornerstone of my upbringing.

Summers in Washington Heights were a sensory feast—hot and loud, with the air pulsating with the rhythms of merengue and bachata. The streets buzzed with life as children played, vendors called out their goods, and neighbors gathered outside, turning the sidewalks into communal living rooms.

Left: Wildy's parents on the A Train, NYC 1980. Right: Wildy and her mom NYC, 1984.

A pivotal moment in my early years came at the age of six during a routine shopping trip with my mother. As we turned the corner on 176th Street, I was captivated by the grand opening of a new clothing boutique. The scene was straight out of a movie—a red ribbon cutting ceremony, a crowd of excited onlookers, and, most memorably, a spinning mannequin adorned in a dazzling sequin dress. That dress, shimmering and elegant, ignited something within me. I was mesmerized, and in that instant, I knew I wanted to create, draw, and wear beautiful dresses.

My family recognized and nurtured my budding talent. To this day, my mom tells stories about my independence when it came to picking out my own outfits and expressing myself through clothing and accessories. She says I inherited the gift for fashion from her mother, my grandmother Ines, who was a very popular fashion designer and seamstress in the Dominican Republic. My parents also gifted me a Barbie light box, a simple yet transformative tool that allowed me to trace fashion illustrations and design paper doll dresses. I loved my light box so much and had it for years, at one point held together with electrical tape.

Through these formative years, filled with familial support, cultural richness, and early artistic endeavors, I really didn't see any examples or role models in my own neighborhood. In the late 1990s, inner cities like Washington Heights were plagued by a huge drug epidemic and teen pregnancies were at an all-time high. It was very normal to see police conducting drug raids outside my window. At a really young age, I decided to go against the grain that I saw around me and sought refuge in my studies, being a straight-A student with a dream of one day being "someone".

Wildy, Age 9, wearing a dress she helped her aunt design and make.

Through these formative years, filled with familial support, cultural richness, and early artistic endeavors, I really didn't see any examples or role models in my own neighborhood. In the late 1990s, inner cities like Washington Heights were plagued by a huge drug epidemic and teen pregnancies were at an all-time high. It was very normal to see police conducting drug raids outside my window. At a really young age, I decided to go against the grain that I saw around me and sought refuge in my studies, being a straight-A student with a dream of one day being "someone".

My favorite uncle, Narciso, played a pivotal role in my childhood. He was my confidant, mentor, and biggest supporter. His passing when I was 14 left a void, but his influence continued to shape my path. He had a deep appreciation for higher education and creativity, encouraging me to explore and express myself and excel in everything I put my mind to. It was he who helped me write my entrance essay for the high school of my dreams, and by the age of 13, I had secured a spot at Fashion Industries High School, a specialized school where I could immerse myself in the world of fashion. There, I learned to sketch, sew, and create entire collections. I was now surrounded by teachers, mentors, and role models, which I really desired to have especially during those formative years.

I'm not sure if it's because I am kind of the middle child—with the typical middle child overachiever behavior—but I always felt a strong drive to excel. I am one of four siblings, with two younger brothers and an older sister, and living in a small apartment for many years made it interesting—we were constantly fighting for space. It's funny because when we talk about our upbringing, it almost feels like we grew up in different homes. Perhaps it's due to the age differences and our diverse circles of friends.

One thing we can all agree on is that my dad kept things exciting and made our house the place where all our friends and cousins would hang out. My mother worked so hard, but we never went without a home-cooked meal. She would often tell people, "I never have to worry about Wildy; she always does so well in school." I'm not sure if that set an unspoken standard for me, but I felt like I couldn't afford to fail. I became, and still am, very hard on myself.

Each of my siblings seemed to be navigating their own worlds, and I refused to be the one to ruffle any feathers. I didn't want to add to my parents' stress, and I had a goal to be the first in my family to graduate from college and pursue my dreams of working in Fashion.

This determination to succeed, coupled with the desire to avoid being a burden, shaped my behavior and work ethic. It pushed me to strive for excellence in everything I did and set the foundation for my future achievements.

The Digital Leap

Graduating with honors from high school earned me a scholarship to attend Syracuse University for their Fine Arts program with a focus on Fashion Design. I was thrilled at the prospect of finally leaving our tiny apartment and having some "space" of my own. In my excitement, I even overlooked my scholarships and acceptance to the Fashion Institute of Technology (FIT), the most prestigious design university next to Parsons. In my mind, I thought, why would I want four more years on 28th Street, four more years of taking the train from the Bronx to the city? By that time, my parents had recently closed on a house in the Bronx. The Bronx! We technically had our own rooms, but I was convinced I would be long gone to Syracuse before the move.

Wildy starting off her Fashion Design career.

Then one day, I received a letter in the mail saying that I didn't have any room and boarding in Syracuse because they had never received my paperwork. This meant I had nowhere to stay. I was faced with a dilemma: either skip a semester and reapply for dorms or reconsider FIT. Looking back now, the urgency of wanting my own independence from my family and our tight quarters had me short-sighted. I can't believe I almost missed out on attending the best design school in the country just because I wanted to be away from "the block." I think it was definitely fate that the paperwork was misplaced.

My first semester at FIT was a breeze because I came from a high school that specialized in fashion. I was so ahead of all the other students. My peers were from all over the world; this was their dream school, their top choice. And here I was, jealous because they got to stay in the dorms while I had to commute to the Bronx. I literally got mugged the first night walking home from school in front of our new house.

By the second semester, my peers had caught up with me, and that's when my competitive spirit was born. We all worked so hard, but I could hear my mother on the phone telling all my aunts, "Oh, Wildy, she's the best in her class," and that became my new standard. I wanted to be the top of my class; I wanted to sketch the best, drape the best, sew the best. I never got less than an A in all my specialized classes. But since FIT was a state university, we also had to write papers and take required state courses like science, math, and history. So there I was, completely immersed in school. If I wasn't writing a paper, I was sewing in my little design studio my parents made for me in the TV room behind our couch. I took summer classes too so that during the regular semester, I wasn't drowning in classes. I would take the maximum number of classes per semester, and towards my senior year, I had to get a part time job as a receptionist on weekends to help with my phone bill, books, and expenses.

Four years later, in 2006, I graduated Magna Cum Laude with a bachelor's degree in fine arts. I received grants, was on the dean's list, and was awarded "The Next Up and Coming Latina Designer" by New York Magazine and El Diario (a very popular magazine back then). I had achieved my goal of graduating college, and at that time, I was the first in my family to do so. I remember it like it was yesterday. My dad told me to take the summer off after college before I started my career. I used to go back to the campus and sit outside because I just didn't know what else to do. I have a memory of sitting outside module D, looking up at the sky, and saying, "I know there is more for me," because in that moment, I had a void. Looking back now, I wish I could tell myself to celebrate, to enjoy, to be in the moment, to take it all in. But instead, I wondered what was in store for me next.

In September after graduation, I landed my first real job as a Design Assistant in the Womenswear division for a very well-known company. I had a small desk in a shared office with three other associate designers. My role was to assist them; I organized the print closet, managed the sample room, and helped tweak designs in Adobe Illustrator. One day, the director came in and handed me ten jacket samples, asking me to CAD them by the next day. I wasn't as fast as the other girls, and they refused to help me. One of them even laughed at me. This was my first taste of the real world. I was confused by the need to sketch existing styles and taken aback by how competitive and catty my co-workers were.

The next day, the director called me into his office and accused me of lying. He said I had written down that I was knowledgeable in CAD in my resume, which I was, but not as quick as the others (yet). He then told me that the other designers were complaining about how I didn't even know how to file their prints properly. I felt warm tears fall from my eyes as I shrunk down in the chair in his office.

Thankfully, because this was a big corporation, it had a well-equipped HR department. A few days later, I was placed under the supervision of the creative director as a temporary solution. She took me under her wing and taught me everything about color analysis, trend forecasting, market research, how to create concept boards on a larger scale, and how to design my own prints.

By then, I had started looking for another job because I wanted to be more hands-on and design clothes, and I was offered a position as an Assistant Designer at a startup for a women's apparel company. When I went to give my notice, the creative director brought me into her office and said that she had spoken to HR and created a position just for me to be her assistant. I would be traveling around the world with her, shopping for the latest fashion trends, and learning from her. Despite this tempting offer, I ended up taking the design job at the smaller company because I wanted a more hands-on design experience.

I stayed in my second job for seven years and established myself as an athleisure designer. I was there when the velour jumpsuits became a thing and launched one of the first activewear brands for Saks. By 2013, I was burnt out from working long hours and the pressure of being on top of trends. I was burnt out from fast fashion and was feeling that void again. I decided to quit after so many years, with no plans and pennies in savings. I couldn't go on. I was sick and had developed an autoimmune disease called Vitiligo, which caused me to start losing the melanin on my hands at first. I was also developing an ulcer in my stomach. It wasn't just my job; at that time, I was going through a lot of changes in my personal life and was about to collapse. I was staying with my parents, who had built an apartment for me in their attic. So there I was, a 25-year-old living in her parents' attic, living "the dream". I was going through an identity crisis too. I had been called "la diseñadora" (the designer) all my life, and now I wasn't, and I didn't know who I was without the title. A few months later, I was restless, and many of my friends would ask me for styling advice. So, I started a personal styling business that didn't go anywhere since I was charging "pay what you can" prices.

However, one of the women I helped style and who attended one of my "Fashion Favor with Wildy" events connected me with the founder of a clothing brand. They partnered with an organization that not only rescues women from sex trafficking in Nepal but also restores them back to society and learn trade skills like sewing. I fell in love with the mission and said yes. I started out helping with styling, then freelance designing, and I even traveled to Nepal and met some of the survivors. It was truly life changing. I continued freelancing for this missional clothing brand on and off as I climbed up the Fashion Corporate Ladder at the same time. Eventually, I got furloughed from both due to the economic crisis and pandemic aftermath.

Wildy walking out with one of her models during a Fashion Show.

By this time, I was living in North Carolina. I was applying for remote design positions and even applied to a few fashion companies in Charlotte, but nothing came through. I decided to start illustrating again—I always went back to art when coping with hard seasonal changes. This time, I decided to share my work online, and people started to ask me if I was selling my art as prints. I would email the files and ask for $50 per download; very organic I did not even have a website. That's when I received a phone call from a family member who said, "Hey, you should really look into NFTs".

The Web 3 Awakening - What the heck is an NFT?

One of the first rules in the NFT and Web3 community is DYOR—do your own research—and that's exactly what I did. I went down the rabbit hole, as I'm sure many of us did. I would listen to Gary Vee speak about it, signed up for NFT 101 courses on Udemy, and finally joined a group called "Krypto Club" on Slack, which was led by my friend TJ, a former Wall Street finance guru. Krypto Club was a place where I could ask questions and learn about the different cryptocurrencies at the time. I opened my first MetaMask wallet and contributed to the NFT conversation.

Awards for her NFTs

Soon after, I joined what we call Web3 Twitter and started participating in various NFT communities like World of Women, Meta Angels, Eyes of Fashion, and other projects that focused on women, art, and fashion. NFT conversations were everywhere, and one day, I saw an ad on Instagram for an NFT marketplace that was pro-artist. This platform helped traditional artists and illustrators onboard into Web3, minting artworks onto the blockchain. The marketplace was crypto-optional, growing quickly, and offered very high royalties back to the creators.

I decided to try it out and minted my first NFT collection of fashion portraits. I was in for a wild ride. Once my work was minted, I was plugged into the community 24/7. It felt like I was thrown into marketing and had to learn very quickly how to talk about my work, my art, and why collectors needed to collect my pieces. A few weeks after minting my work and having it collected, it hit the secondary market, and overnight I made over a thousand dollars in royalties.

I felt so empowered for the first time in a long time. Web3 represented a shift towards a more user-centric internet, where individuals have greater control and ownership over their digital lives, and where transparency and trust are enhanced through decentralized technologies. For an artist, this means global reach, direct monetization and ownership, innovation and experimentation, and inclusivity and representation.

Community and engagement are some of the most powerful tools that Web3 offers. With well-established artists joining this new digital art movement alongside emerging artists, it created an even plain field. We were all artists trying to help each other out. This allowed for networking to be established in a magnified way. You could directly message an artist you've admired all your life, and it was completely normal to share opportunities, resources, and contacts with one another.

As Gary Vee predicted, NFTs, like every technological advancement, were bound to experience a bubble burst. Projects started to decline in sales, and the celebrity hype around them began to lose its sparkle. For one-of-one artists like myself, this wasn't necessarily a bad thing. The decline left only those who passionately believed in the power of creator ownership. To stay relevant, we all had to dig deeper as artists and rediscover our "why."

At least, that's what I did. I created a digital illustration, a fashion NFT, of a woman with flowers in her hair and vitiligo on her skin. This piece was called "Wildflower 38"—my vitiligo genesis piece. It was the piece that gave me my voice, freedom, and stance as an artist. I shared my story about how my vitiligo was spreading, but that I didn't want to hide it anymore.

The response from the community was impactful. I received message after message from others with vitiligo who felt represented and seen. This was when I discovered The Art of Self Embrace. I started to combine my fashion art, advocacy for vitiligo, and personal story, which launched my brand, Wildflower Fields. Wildflower Fields is a creative movement brand celebrating women and diversity through fashion, art, and innovative storytelling.

NFT NYC 2024

"Wildflower 38," my NFT, was collected by a woman founder in the space whom I admired greatly. Her support and belief in my work and story made me understand the power of vulnerability and authenticity. That collector would soon become the co-founder with Randi Zuckerberg of The Hug, a community that has helped me partner with opportunities that have been life-changing, not just for me but for thousands of other artists like me.

Museum visitors with Wildy's art.

I continued to merge art and technology and was approached by a curator who wanted to showcase my Vitiligo Fashion series in the first-ever NFT Museum in Seattle. There, I exhibited alongside digital fashion artists who were pushing the boundaries. I couldn't believe that I was part of this new movement and started to get more opportunities to exhibit my work, including my first international exhibition in Colombia.

I attended my first NFT NYC in 2023, where my work was featured, and my face was up in Times Square. I also had the honor of being one of the speakers on the "Latinas in NFTs" panel, moderated by one of my mentors, Lucia Diaz. As I sat on the stage inside the Jacob Javits Center, I experienced a full-circle moment. The Javits Center was where my mom retired after working there for 30 years and where I also worked as a receptionist while attending FIT. And here I was, back again, exhibiting my art and speaking on stage.

NFT NYC 2024

Current Ventures

One of the advantages of being in Web3 is that it becomes almost like a big umbrella where creatives can be multifaceted. In traditional work, many creators struggle with marketing themselves because we either put ourselves in a box or others do it for us. Web3 has allowed me to break free from those constraints and explore various avenues of creativity.

I ventured into creating digital art and officially delved into what we call AI art. To be completely honest, I feared it at first. "What do you mean you can tell artificial intelligence what to create by only using words?" I was intrigued, just like when I went down the rabbit hole of NFTs.

I started collaborating with MidJourney but quickly realized that I wasn't getting the results I wanted. MidJourney could not recognize the word "vitiligo" and lacked diversity when the tool first came out. I began digitizing the vitiligo into my AI images and advocated for people who looked like me not to be left out. So, I dove deeper into AI collaborative art and soon learned how to train my own AI models to represent the vitiligo community.

My project, "The Art of Self Embrace: My Vitiligo Journey," was exhibited at The Canvas 3.0 Gallery in NYC. This project not only showcased my work but also highlighted the importance of inclusivity and representation in AI art. By training my AI models to accurately represent the vitiligo community, I aimed to ensure that people with vitiligo could see themselves in the digital art space. This journey has been incredibly fulfilling and has opened up new opportunities for me to continue advocating for diversity in art and technology.

I participated in the first AI Fashion Week in New York City, where hundreds of emerging and experienced designers from around the world collaborated with AI to create a complete fashion show. We had to design the location of the show, the models, the clothing, and make it as cohesive as possible. This was no easy task, considering that within one year, AI capabilities had accelerated at a speed that is mind-blowing. Although I didn't make the finals cut that season, I tried again for Season Two.

By then, I was training my own AI models, which allowed me to be one of the first AI Fashion Designers to have vitiligo representation. This was a huge win for me, and I made it to the top 20 finalists. AI Fashion Week gained significant recognition from Vogue Business and was sponsored by Revolve. The top three winners get to bring their AI creations to real life. The jurors included top industry professionals, such as Norma Kamali.

Once again, Web3 brought me to a full-circle moment where I was now merging my two loves: fashion and now tech. This experience not only showcased the potential of AI in fashion but also emphasized the importance of inclusivity and representation. It was an incredible journey that highlighted how far we can push the boundaries of creativity when we embrace new technologies and stay true to our unique perspectives.

This journey also opened doors for me beyond the fashion world. I was invited to speak at the United Nations 78th Science Summit and join the Women of Web3. I had the honor of speaking on the panel "The Evolution of Art and Fashion with AI and Blockchain," which opened the door for more speaking engagements, workshops, and other amazing opportunities. One of these was working with the historic brand L'Oréal alongside other women artists in the Web3 and AI space. We spoke about how artificial intelligence can enhance the creative process and how it can be used as a tool to materialize and bring our concepts to life.

Wildy speaking at the Women of Web3 session for UNGA78, NYC September 2023.

Wildy speaking to L'Oréal staff about AI tools used in her designs.

This entire experience has been transformative, showcasing not just the future of fashion and technology but also the power of community, representation, and the relentless pursuit of innovation.

Looking Ahead

As an artist in Web3, I want to continue learning, exploring, and approaching technological tools like AI with curiosity and childlike wonder. I feel so blessed to be surrounded by women in the space who are pushing boundaries and paving the way. Women like Claire Silver, who curated one of my AI artworks and has been collaborating with AI since 2018, and Amber Vittoria, who taught me to view my voice and stance as an artist as "this and that" rather than "this OR that." Moving forward, I aim to remain uncompromising with my creative ideas, knowing that if there isn't a way, I can create a whole new way.

Wildy with her son appreciating and creating art.

I am excited about teaching the next generation about the power that lies at the intersection of art and cutting-edge technology. My 7-year-old son is already well-versed in what I do. He creates his own storybooks with ChatGPT and has his art on the blockchain. Seeing his enthusiasm and understanding of these tools at such a young age is incredibly inspiring.

Digital fashion and AI fashion are becoming mainstream, with luxury brands embracing the power behind technologies like AR, VR, and NFC capabilities, and using AI to help achieve sustainability goals. It excites me to see traditional fashion companies like WGSN using AI for campaigns and trend reports. Currently, I am working as a consultant for a traditional fashion company as part of their discovery team. In this role, I act as a bridge, helping onboard the traditional fashion world into the digital age. It's very exciting to be a part of this transformation and to provide a creative perspective on the future of fashion.

Looking ahead, I am eager to see how the convergence of art, fashion, and technology will continue to evolve. I envision a world where artists have unprecedented tools to bring their visions to life, where inclusivity and representation are at the forefront, and where the boundaries of creativity are constantly being expanded. My goal is to remain at the forefront of this movement, continually innovating and inspiring others to explore the endless possibilities that lie ahead.

Conclusion

In this journey, I've embraced the power of change and the necessity of self-belief. From the streets of Washington Heights to the halls of the United Nations, every step of my journey has been marked by resilience, creativity, and a deep commitment to authenticity.

Reflecting on my path, I see a story of transformation. It is a testament to the idea that obstacles can become opportunities and that our greatest challenges often lead to our most profound growth. My experiences have taught me that embracing one's unique identity and talents is not just an act of self-love but a powerful catalyst for innovation and influence.

For those venturing into the Web3 space, my journey serves as a reminder that the future belongs to the curious and the brave. It is a space where technology meets artistry, where community and collaboration are the bedrocks of success, and where inclusivity and representation are not just goals but realities we can achieve together.

As I look to the future, my hope is to inspire the next generation of creators to explore the limitless possibilities at the intersection of art and technology. Let your imagination run wild, stay curious, and never stop embracing your true self.

If my story resonates with you, I invite you to engage further with my work and ideas. Follow me on my journey as I continue to explore and innovate within the realms of art, fashion, and technology. Join the conversation on Web3 and NFTs by connecting with me on social media and participating in community discussions.

To dive deeper into the world of Web3, consider these resources:

- Creating a free artist profile on thehug.xyz and tapping into all of the free resources they offer to artists, as well as open calls for paid opportunities, exhibitions, workshops, and more.
- Books like "The NFT Handbook" by Matt Fortnow and QuHarrison Terry: This book offers comprehensive insights into NFTs and their impact on various industries.
- Web3 Twitter and communities.
- Podcasts like "The GaryVee Audio Experience": Stay updated on the latest trends and insights in the world of NFTs and Web3.

Remember, the world of Web3 is vast and constantly evolving. Stay curious, keep learning, and don't be afraid to explore new horizons. The intersection of art and technology holds endless possibilities, and your unique voice can contribute to shaping the future. Lean into your individuality, unique voice, and authenticity in all that you do. In a field of roses, you are a Wildflower.

Let's Connect

Wildy Martinez
www.womenofweb3un.io/speakers/wildy-martinez

CHAPTER SIX

From the Earth to the Moon: A Journey of Art and Empowerment
By Ana Isabel Rivas Fernández

My name is Ana Isabel Rivas Fernández, I am 32 years old, and I live in the vibrant, crazy and unique set of magic and chaos called Mexico City. This year, 2024 for those reading in the future or in space, has marked a significant milestone in my life, something that just a couple years ago I would've never imagined or even considered it an option: one of my art pieces was sent to the Moon, and a small part of me is now up there, in the that beautiful circle that lights our nights on earth. It's funny because before, the moon was just there, looking gorgeous, and a constant in the sky, today every time I look at it, I don't just see what everyone in the world sees along with me.

Today every time I look at it, I remember how far I've come, all the obstacles beaten, all the times I considered giving up, all the times I wasn't sure as I was as good as I've become and my heart fills with happiness and gratitude for achieving something that once seemed impossible but that my heart always knew it was.

Young Ana without a clue about what was going to happen a couple of decades later.

In my short span on this Earth, I've realized that my purpose in this life is to inspire, to inspire more women to follow their inner light, to feed the fire within, often stifled by the fear of judgment, uncertainty, or failure. It's AMAZING how many reasons there can be to stop us from pursuing a dream, even from trying just because we paralyze ourselves in fear, but I want to share my story about how I transformed my life by leveraging my talents in Web3, and I hope it inspires you, whoever you are reading this, to believe that you can achieve the impossible, the things you never dared imagine, or were never sure you could accomplish.

If you told Ana from ten years ago where I would be right now, and everything that I'm doing, I never would have believed it, because I never imagined where I'd be where I am today.

I grew up in a society that dictates that women must marry and have children, stay at home and be housewives at a certain age to be accepted or reach high corporate positions to be considered successful. I could never fit in that mold, I always felt like I was not destined to follow a standard, and boy was I right. Life has taken me to extraordinary places, revealing new ways to build a full, happy, and magical life that didn't seem to be in the picture before. In recent years, I have learned to define success on my terms, trusting myself and following my instincts. And in doing so I have found fulfillment, joy, inspiration, friends, and different sides of me that were hiding and have come to the light one by one.

Roots and Wings: From Mexico to Blockchain

I was born in Mexico City and spent most of my life in a kind of bubble. I grew up in the southern part of the city and attended the same school until I was 18. My family was not rich, but I never lacked anything. I never had a reason to be hungry and it seemed like it would continue that way until lightning struck. I had the opportunity to move to Buenos Aires, Argentina, to continue my studies at the University of Palermo. This was an adventure, a different country far from my city but sharing the same language, and as the Hero in Joseph Campbell's book, I heard the calling and decided to embark in my own journey.

Leaving my comfort zone was one of the best decisions I ever made. From the moment I started my studies, I began working as a graphic designer at an NGO called BAIS (Buenos Aires International Students). I soon discovered that every concept I learned in class was immediately applied to my work, it was like feeding gas into a fire, which accelerated my professional development and allowed me to gain confidence in myself more quickly, as I was making some money and creating pieces with design that seemed to matter.

Argentina, Bariloche 2013, traveling with BAIS as a travel staff

At BAIS, I not only served as a designer, but also coordinated events and trips for the community of international students in Argentina. This experience brought me closer to people from all over the world, opening a lot of doors in my brain and allowing me to learn about different cultures and, at the same time, discover more bits and pieces of myself in the process, on a personal and professional level.

At the University, I specialized in Graphic Design, Corporate Image, and Advertising Creativity. Studying in Argentina, renowned for its creativity in the advertising world, was a transformative experience. Although I have always carried Mexico in my veins, Argentina has earned a place in my heart for broadening my perspective, enhancing my creativity, and providing the tools necessary to believe in my abilities and explore horizons beyond what I thought was within reach.

In 2016, I graduated with a thesis on 3D brands that was considered innovative at the time. It explored the idea of how brands could adopt three-dimensional forms that would apply to communicate in various contexts. Without knowing it, I was ahead of concepts that I now see materialized in projects like NFTs and the Metaverse. I just started to see the light that would turn into a magical sun.

After graduating, I returned home to Mexico City in 2016 and went back to the traditional system. I had already escaped a bit clueless to it happening, but never being comfortable in it. I had a couple of jobs, however, deep down I always knew that my creativity and ideas did not fit that typical system and mold.

Over time, I realized that I needed to acquire new skills to advance my professional career. I tried learning as much as possible taking different courses on Brand Management, Data Analysis, SEO, and Digital Strategies to improve my profile and expand my reach professionally.

It was in 2021, during the pandemic, that I discovered NFTs (Non-Fungible Tokens) and experienced a radical transformation in my life, perspective and my work. These digital assets not only piqued my curiosity but also expanded my vision of the creative and financial possibilities in the digital space with a bit of creativity not only at creating art but distributing it and giving it meaning well beyond just being appreciated.

With my background in Design and my newfound passion for data,

NFTs made sense to several of my ideas that previously had no structure. The ability to store files on Blockchain and connect with a global community opened incredible new opportunities. And that was only the beginning.

The Digital Leap - Falling Down the Rabbit Hole

The expression "falling down the rabbit hole" is frequently used in the crypto world because many of us have experienced the process of how we started out of curiosity, exploring the world of Web3, and suddenly found ourselves completely immersed in a universe that seems endless. What began as curiosity, quickly became a deep dive into new technologies, protocols, and communities that transform our perception of the digital space as we know it and how it can be used for infinite more purposes.

In 2021, I started designing NFTs as a hobby, but it swiftly and surprisingly became a source of income in cryptocurrencies. This change marked my life; I went from having a conventional job to calling myself a crypto artist, selling my art and creativity on Blockchain to fellow crypto heads that appreciated it and understood more than anyone in the "real" world would've. This new path not only transformed my professional perspective but also introduced me to a new world where creativity merges with technology, offering new forms of artistic expression and financial diversification.

My Mexican Calaveritas version of Bored Apes, created in 2022.

Art on Blockchain represents an evolution compared to traditional art in terms of ownership, authenticity, and traceability. Each work is immutably recorded on the blockchain, ensuring its authenticity and allowing artists to receive direct royalties without going through the hoops of galleries, art dealers, or just curious eyes that waste time. This process eliminates intermediaries and democratizes access to digital art, providing creators with a platform where, for the first time, they can interact directly with their global audience, without geographical barriers. This transparency and decentralization not only make a new aspect of the art market possible but also create opportunities for artistic expression in a secure and reliable environment.

Initially, I found it difficult to communicate my ideas and connect with people who understood what I was talking about. My preferred social network is Instagram, and when I shared information on these topics, I often felt that my followers were not interested, and my posts fell into a void, with heartless likes at best, and being ignored at worst. Although I was frequently advised to join Spaces on X to expand my network, I resisted, I liked my bubble on Instagram, had a solid base of followers and it was simply what I knew pretty well.

At that time, my experience was limited to working with intermediaries who commissioned very specific designs and handled the sale of my works, depending on them showing it and pushing it. However, I was very curious about understanding the entire sales process. I wanted to know who the collectors were and how this new market operated. Curiosity led me to delve deeper into the ecosystem, seeking direct connections with buyers and exploring the possibilities of personally connecting with the global community of decentralization enthusiasts.

In 2022, I moved to Phoenix, Arizona, where I had the time I needed to connect with the X platform. Gradually, I found this community that spoke the same language as me. Since then, my posts have made sense because I found the right people. They say content is King, but context is Queen indeed. And more importantly, distribution is the kingdom.

A crucial event in my development was attending NFTNYC in 2022. I had the opportunity to meet the people behind the profile picture cartoons, the protocols, and the marketplaces I interacted with online on a daily basis. These people were my new heroes, the creators and movers that I admired, and they did not disappoint. On top of that, I connected with prominent Latin American leaders in the crypto space, who not only shared their experience and knowledge with me, but also gave me new life and put the gust of wind I needed under my newly grown wings deeply inspiring me and encouraging me to create my personal brand: Ananá.

NFT NYC 2022, Latin Web3 entrepreneurs

It was then that I realized I didn't know anyone in Mexico who was going through the same thing as me. Despite having a lot of valuable information, I didn't know what to do with it. At that moment, I thought about how useful it would have been to have someone guide me when I started, to have that mentor that the hero needed. In the absence of my own mentor, I decided to become that person for me and others, using my experience to help those taking their first steps in this world. My goal is to share my story and what I've learned to make the path easier for others in this exciting and sometimes complicated adventure.

When I returned to Mexico from New York City, I decided to put my plans into action. I organized local meetups to connect with the community and teach others about NFTs and their wonderful world. I invited influential people with successful projects as speakers to share their experiences and answer our questions; to shine a light in the dark tunnel we were very eager to travel. These events were crucial in resolving our doubts and learning from success stories, inspiring us to give it a bigger shot in the space.

Devcon Bogotá, Colombia 2023. Picture taken after a 21-hour hackathon developing Web3 solutions MX🦋 Proudly representing Mexican women in the space.

Additionally, I began participating as a speaker at Web3 events, teaching both in-person and online classes, and started a podcast to establish myself as a reference figure in Mexico and Latin America on topics like NFTs, the Metaverse, and Blockchain given that there was very little content in Spanish. This commitment has allowed me not only to share knowledge but also to strengthen the community and promote the growth of this exciting niche in Mexico and Spanish speaking countries.

At the beginning of 2023, I had the opportunity to collaborate with Bright Moments, a DAO-driven art gallery, to organize an exhibition showcasing both global and local artists in Mexico City. This collaboration was particularly significant as it allowed us to open the first gallery dedicated to NFTs in Mexico, located in the eclectic Roma neighborhood. These events not only promoted digital art and technological innovation in the city but also served as a community hub to foster dialogue between creators, collectors, and digital art enthusiasts worldwide.

One night at Thursday's community meetup in Bright Moments CDMX Art Gallery, 2023.

While actively participating in in-person events, I also focused on developing my digital presence. I kept my profile updated and took advantage of every art call that resonated with me. Gradually, my efforts began to bear fruit. Over time, my personal brand gained recognition, and I started to be acknowledged in the digital art and NFT sphere as an expert. Opportunities began to come naturally, without me having to actively seek them and it snowballed into an avalanche that has taken me to incredible places.

That's how I ended up participating in the BitBassel and Space Blue call, and just you wait until you read about it.

The Web 3 Awakening - Ojitos lindos to the Moon

At the end of 2022, I participated in the BitBasel 3rd Annual CryptoArt for Impact Challenge, representing one of the United Nations Sustainable Development Goals (SDGs), in an initiative in collaboration with Space Blue. The objective was to create a digital collectible that represented one of these Goals through a social impact project.

My artwork titled "Beautiful Eyes" was selected as the winner and represents SDG #3, Good Health and Well-being. The funds from the sale of this piece will be used to pay for my mother's cataract surgery. As part of the prize, my piece was exhibited during Miami Art Basel, and this year, on February 15th, it was sent to the Moon, literally.

Ananá holding Ojitos Lindos, a digital copy of this art piece is on the moon.

Nearly a year passed from the time we received the news until Falcon finally launched. Those months were filled with uncertainty, eagerness and the imposter syndrome took over whenever I let my guard down. It was a dark time, and it took a toll simply because I couldn't really understand that I was part of that, that a piece of me was going into space, and that me, Ana, Ananá, was chosen for this amazing project. It was the first time since 1972 that something was sent to the Moon, and a piece of my digital art was inside? I couldn't believe it, it was incredible.

The messages from the Universe come to us in surprising ways, but this one truly exceeded all my expectations. "Ojitos Lindos (Beautiful Eyes)" is more than a piece of art on the Moon; it represents an awakening in my life and a story that God gave me to share with those around me. "Ojitos Lindos" is hope and revolution within a centralized and traditional world. "Ojitos Lindos" is confidence in my inner fire, in following my instincts, and letting myself be guided by my intuition.

"Ojitos Lindos" is now part of the Lunaprise Moon Museum, a collection of 222 pieces that were engraved on a nickel disc sent within the Lunar Lander called Odysseus. It launched from Kennedy Space Center and landed on the Moon on February 22, 2024.

Official Space Blue Artis ID, number 30. Ananá is 1 of 222 humans on earth that made history by having their art sent to the Moon.

Even today, after being there to witness the launch, it feels like a dream. I've always had a special connection with the Moon. A few years ago, I read a book called *Moonology* that served as an evolutionary springboard for me, as I was able to synchronize my life with the phases of the Moon, and I know that somehow, that had something to do with me being chosen to be one of 222 humans in a world out of billions and billions.

Sending a tiny piece of my digital art to the Moon filled me with excitement, happiness, gratitude, satisfaction, empowerment, and many other emotions that I would never have found in a traditional job.

Web3, for me, is this new space where anything is possible, from sending art to the Moon to participating in the first UN women's session discussing blockchain and the decentralized future. It's an opportunity to be part of many firsts, and to help change the world.

Current Ventures - Guiding Light

In 2023, Sandy Martinez kindly invited me to be part of Women of Web3, a group of 17 female leaders, creators, and developers representing gender equity in Web3 through the Sustainable Development Goals 5 and 10, which champion gender equality and the reduction of inequalities.

Women of Web3 was the first group of women to speak about blockchain and the decentralized future in a United Nations Session during the UNGA78 in New York City, another dream come true.

Once again, I could never have imagined speaking at the United Nations, but Sandy and Cyndi made it possible. There is something very magical about the people I have met in Web3: they have big dreams, many of which I didn't even know I had until they popped before my eyes, and I recognized them, took them and made the best of them.

So, in September last year, 17 women met in New York to broadcast our session from the World Trade Center, where each of us shared experiences, expertise, current use cases, and different strategies that positioned us within a traditionally male-dominated niche. We had the chance to show the world we were rule benders, we were creators without limits, and we were here to show everyone that women can rule, change, and lead.

That trip also transformed my life forever, and my artist's heart felt very inspired when I started to get to know these women, spend time with them, and learn so much from them in such a short time. Knowledge just comes through your pores when you are willing to learn and are inspired by those teaching.

I knew from the start that what we were doing was a historic event that deserved to be immortalized on the blockchain. That's when I came up with the idea of creating an NFT that would tell our story, represent the context of our session at the UN, include the women who were part of it, and allow the community to feel involved with our mission.

Women Of Web 3 at BitBasel event celebrating their participation on UNGA78

Our NFT was titled "Guiding Light" and stands as a powerful symbol of unity, sisterhood, and empowerment. This art piece encapsulates the beautiful journeys of women from across the globe as they trace their paths on the Blockchain. Using one-of-a-kind artwork as a digital tool, we aimed to connect with individuals on a profound level.

Guiding Light, first NFT representing a United Nations Session, 2023. Creative Strategy and background by Ananá, 3D and Motion Graphics by Soho.

The artwork showcased the 17 female leaders, creators, and developers in the Web3 industry who participated in the UNGA 78. It was an open edition that was sold during our time in New York for the United Nations Session, priced at 0.01111 ETH, and we sold 95 of them. By purchasing this NFT, people helped us raise 1.03 ETH, with 100% of the profits going towards scholarships for Science, Technology, Engineering, and Mathematics courses for girls and teenagers.

Additionally, we built a Metaverse in Spatial, where our community could enter to buy our NFT with crypto or a credit card, creating a space to interact directly with them and have a place that encapsulates the essence of that event forever in the Metaverse.

We took advantage of this incredible event to demonstrate how Web 3 is the digital future, using some tools that allow us to create small but significant changes. "Guiding Light" is the perfect use case we needed to share the benefits of NFTs from a more user-friendly perspective.

Women of Web 3 Metaverse experience, live in Spatial.io.

Blockchain is the foundation on which the digital future will be built. It provides traceability, transparency, and decentralization to any process that needs or benefits from these capabilities.

This project not only gave me the opportunity to bring to life those ideas I had in my head, which all became a reality, but it also surrounded me with incredible women who have become mentors, friends, sisters, partners, advisors, and any kind of support I've needed since I met them.

There is nothing more powerful than a group of women who decided to go after their dreams and meet to create opportunities.

Looking Ahead

I haven't always had my next steps clear, but once I dedicated myself to this mission, life has put me in the right places with the right people. Currently, I am working in a large corporation; once again, I entered the system, but now I feel fulfilled. I do not seek recognition in this position because I have given it to myself with my personal brand, achieving my own goals, and fulfilling my dreams. I feel grateful for the experience I'm living right now and I'm learning a whole new world of e-commerce.

I always find a good reason to tell these stories to people. I feel so grateful to Web3 that I will tell them as many times as necessary because I know there is a young woman like me a few years ago who is looking for some answers that I can give her.

I will continue to follow my intuition to connect with the divine plan of the Universe, trusting that each step guides me towards a greater purpose. By allowing my intuition to lead, I honor my own essence and create a clear path for those around me. This journey is not mine alone; it is an invitation for others to join and discover their own potential. By sharing my experiences and insights, I hope to inspire others to listen to their inner voice and trust in their ability to achieve their dreams.

Ananá holding the Mexican flag at Cape Canaveral on February 14, 2024, at Kennedy Space Center. One day before the launch.

Conclusion

Building on these transformative experiences, I am dedicated to inspiring and empowering women to embrace their potential and pursue their dreams fearlessly. By sharing my journey and the possibilities within Web 3, I hope to illuminate the path for others, fostering a community that thrives on innovation, decentralization, and gender equality.

My involvement in groundbreaking initiatives and collaborations continues to fuel my mission to support STEM education and create lasting social impact through art and technology. I look forward to the endless possibilities that lie ahead, eager to contribute to the digital future that is already here.

Reflection

Blockchain has taken me to the Moon, awakened my mind, expanded my opportunities, allowing me to understand and apply innovative technology to improve processes and create a more transparent and decentralized future. It has allowed me to develop in a new industry where more women are urgently needed, and I want to share these opportunities with everyone who reads this.

I am very proud to be a Mexican woman who has a place in these pages. I hope my story resonates with you, that you find in me a mirror reflecting what you can achieve and be here.

Let's Connect

Ana Isabel Rivas Fernández
www.womenofweb3un.io/speakers/ana-isabel-rivas

ADVISORS CORNER

Envisioning Inclusive Futures: The Power of Women in Web3
By Cyndi Coon

My journey into the Web3 space is rooted in my boundless curiosity, shaped by my background as a creative and a futurist. My imagination naturally reaches far into the future, allowing me to grasp the immense potential that Web3 holds for humanity. When I discuss Web3, I'm not merely referring to blockchain, cryptocurrencies, or NFTs—though these are significant elements still in their infancy. Instead, I envision Web3 as a transformative force that enables unparalleled personalization, empowering individuals to control and own their data.

In the future, people will no longer unknowingly sign away their digital lives in fine print. Instead, they will consciously decide if and how they wish to share or monetize their data. This shift will democratize financial opportunities, enabling every individual to earn in ways previously unimaginable.

As technology advances, much of our work may be automated by AI agents and bots. However, the true value humans will possess lies in their minds, personal data and information—an asset that Web3 will allow us to recognize and capitalize on. This belief is the cornerstone of my passion for Web3, driven by my focus as a human-centric futurist.

My partnership with Sandy Martinez epitomizes this passion. We connected at Arizona State University, where her leadership and commitment to community deeply resonated with me. Our shared dedication to human well-being quickly led to collaboration on a project that combined our big dreams and aspirations. One of Sandy's goals was to speak at the United Nations (UN). With my experience in organizing programs during the UN General Assembly (UNGA) Science Summit, I knew we could achieve this.

Cyndi's UNGA78 Announcement

Together, Sandy and I crafted a proposal focusing on women in Web3, grounded in my belief that when women achieve economic prosperity, the entire community—and indeed, the world—benefits. We assembled a diverse group of women, shared our stories, and strategized our participation at the UNGA in September 2023. Our efforts culminated in an extraordinary day at the Oculus Trade Center in New York City, where each woman shared her vision for the future of Web3.

The event's success solidified my commitment to be an advisor to Sandy as she launched the Women in Web3 organization. As an advisor and advocate, I continue to champion the inclusion of female voices in the Web3 space at the UNGA and far beyond. I am deeply committed to amplifying the voices of the remarkable women who contributed to this movement, ensuring that their stories are not only heard but celebrated.

The creation of this book is a testament to that commitment. The women featured here are experts and pioneers, and their names deserve to be known. As you read their stories, I hope you are inspired by their dedication to their communities and the future of Web3. These women have the vision to see the invisible, the courage to pursue it, and the leadership to bring it into reality. They are the true voices of the future in Web3.

Cyndi Coon is a Web 3.0 Advisor, a time traveler, a rule-bender, nerding out for good using data, science and curious questions as an Applied Futurist, AI Adventurer, Experiential Researcher, and Speaker.

Let's Connect

Cyndi Coon
www.womenofweb3un.io/speakers/cyndi-coon
Linktree: linktr.ee/cyndicoon

ADVISORS CORNER

Building Bridges: Championing Diversity and Inclusive Futures in the Blockchain Space
By Mauricio Cruz

I am Mauricio Cruz, I am 44 years old, and I come from a world where there was no internet, no social media, no streaming services like Netflix or Spotify. I've witnessed firsthand the transformation of technology over the past 40 years and its profound impact on society. Among these transformative technologies, blockchain stands out to me as revolutionary—a force that can change the world. I saw this potential immediately, recognizing it as a tool to fight for freedom and human rights, enabling a market free from government control and intermediaries.

After 22 years in the industry of smart buildings, helping companies save energy and reduce costs, I decided to shift my focus entirely to the Web3 space. My journey into technology began at a young age, growing up with computers when they were still in their infancy. Over the years, I've witnessed the evolution from text-based interfaces to the sophisticated, visually engaging systems we have today. This deep understanding of technology, coupled with my passion for innovation, led me to the blockchain industry, where I now focus on fostering growth and adoption in Latin America, particularly in the Spanish-speaking community.

In this chapter, I'll delve into my journey as a leader in the Web3 space, with a particular emphasis on supporting women in this rapidly evolving industry.

I firmly believe that the fastest way to accelerate the adoption of Web3 is by closing the gender gap. Throughout my life, I've seen women excel in STEAM fields, often outperforming their male counterparts. By empowering more women to join and thrive in Web3, we can create a more inclusive, innovative, and equitable future for everyone.

Role in the Web3 Community

My role in the Web3 community is deeply rooted in generating value for the Hispanic and Latino markets. As a content creator and advisor, I have hosted over 100 Twitter Spaces, focusing on Web3 technologies. In these spaces, I consistently invite women to share their insights, such as Lucía Iturriaga, a remarkable lawyer who co-hosts with me on a regular basis. Our collaboration in "La Abogada y el Ingeniero" has been instrumental in amplifying her voice in the Web3 ecosystem.

Since October 2022, I have been organizing in-person events across Monterrey and other parts of Mexico, with the support of the mxweb3 community and other networks. These events provide an essential platform for individuals to learn about Web3, connect with like-minded people, and explore opportunities to form teams and start businesses. One of the key figures in these efforts is Berenice Ruiz, a dynamic entrepreneur who leads our community's initiatives, fostering collaborations with universities and blockchain groups.

Through these initiatives, I have seen firsthand the importance of creating inclusive environments, particularly for women in the Web3 space. Our commitment to inclusivity in all events and community activities has not only increased engagement but also strengthened our collective understanding of Web3 dynamics, ensuring that diverse perspectives are represented in the ongoing evolution of this technology.

How to Support Women in Web3

Empowering women in Web3 has always been one of the key drivers of my work. One of the ways I've supported this mission is through mentorship and networking. I've worked closely with companies like Vadi, led by Natalia Cueto, where I'm not only a partner but also an active supporter of their mission to empower women and girls in blockchain and STEAM careers. Vadi offers workshops, conferences, and educational events, and our collaboration has helped create opportunities for women to connect with experts and the broader crypto community. Additionally, I've supported and mentored female leaders in the industry, fostering relationships that empower women to take on leadership roles in Web3.

Mauricio Cruz and Natalia Cueto in Blockchain Land, Monterrey Oct 2022

I've also championed female-led projects by offering support and collaboration. For example, I've actively supported Nohbek, a blockchain security platform led by Jazmin García and Brenda

Cuevas. Our friendship and professional relationship have been mutually beneficial, as we've helped each other grow in this ecosystem. Whether through connecting them with valuable contacts, inviting them to speak at significant events, or collaborating on initiatives, my goal has always been to amplify their impact and visibility in the Web3 space.

My collaboration with Sandy Martinez and Women of Web3 (WW3) has been particularly impactful. I met Sandy through Twitter Spaces, and was immediately impressed by her dedication and leadership in Web3. She invited me to serve as an advisor for WW3, and I've supported their initiatives, including the significant participation in the United Nations 78th Science Summit.

My involvement ranged from content creation and promotion to collaborating with Ana Isabel Rivas in planning the NFT collection to celebrate the UN Science Summit and coordinating with platforms for the successful launch. WW3 is a transformative movement that aligns with the Sustainable Development Goals (SDGs) 5 and 10, focusing on gender equality and reducing inequalities. I'm proud to contribute to their mission by elevating female leaders and fostering gender inclusivity in the Web3 space.

How to Serve as an Ally in Developing Web3

To serve as an effective ally in the Web3 space, active engagement and advocacy are crucial. My approach to being an ally involves not only advocating for gender equality and inclusivity but also directly supporting women in Web3 by amplifying their voices, promoting their work, and investing in their growth. One of the most impactful ways I do this is by supporting the niches within Web3 that resonate with me, particularly the digital art sector.

I firmly believe that digital art, in its various forms, is playing a pivotal role in attracting more people to this industry. Personally, I find immense joy in collecting art from emerging artists who are in the process of building their reputations, influence, and reach. Being part of their journey by collecting their work, offering advice on the tools to use, and giving them personal mentorship is incredibly rewarding.

I've built strong friendships with many artists, both men and women, who are at the forefront of the Web3 art scene. This dynamic, burgeoning industry is thrilling to be a part of, as we witness different individuals rise to prominence. For instance, following and supporting the careers of artists like Ana Isabel Rivas and Amaranta Martinez has been nothing short of spectacular. Watching their growth in the industry and being a part of their stories by collecting their art, helping to promote their work, and assisting in expanding their reach has been a mutually beneficial experience.

Amaranta Martinez, Ana Isabel Rivas, Chica Web3, Mauricio Cruz in Times Square Apr 2024

For the artist, selling their art and gaining wider recognition is invaluable. For the collector, there is not only the potential for the artwork to appreciate in value as the artist becomes more famous, but there's also the satisfaction of contributing to the success of someone whose work and vision you believe in. It's a win-win for everyone involved.

One of my most meaningful collaborations has been with Sol Siete, a talented artist from Buenos Aires. I had the pleasure of supporting her in gaining recognition in Mexico by investing in bringing her training program and inviting her to participate in a hackathon where we were able to collaborate and win. This experience, in my opinion, transformed her perspective on what is possible in this space and what she can achieve.

Spending nearly a month together in Mexico allowed me to get to know her better and learn a great deal about the music industry. She, in turn, taught me about the numerous advantages that Web3 technology offers to independent musicians. After delivering a course for musicians in Monterrey, she went on to give the same course in Mexico City and has since returned to Buenos Aires. However, I believe that this journey has significantly propelled her personal and professional projects within the Web3 space.

Sol Siete, Mauricio Cruz in mxweb3, crypto hub in Monterrey

Through these experiences, I have come to understand that being an ally is not just about offering support from the sidelines—it's about actively engaging, building relationships, and creating opportunities for those you believe in. By investing my time, resources, and expertise in the growth of women in Web3, I hope to contribute to a more inclusive, innovative, and equitable future for everyone in this rapidly evolving industry.

In reflecting on my journey of supporting women in Web3, it becomes clear that allyship and active engagement are crucial in building a more diverse and innovative blockchain landscape. By embracing our roles within the community and promoting inclusivity, we can contribute to a Web3 space that is not only healthier and more abundant but also more equitable for everyone. My hope is that this chapter serves as an inspiration for new innovators to join this movement and help shape the future of technology.

I invite you to join the mxweb3 community in Monterrey or connect with a local Web3 community near you. I also encourage you to attend in-person events, seek out opportunities to collaborate, and focus on building diverse teams. By working together and supporting women in this industry, we can drive meaningful change and create a thriving ecosystem for all.

Let's Connect

Mauricio Cruz
www.linkedin.com/in/mauriciocruzcpp/

ADVISORS CORNER

From Colorful Walls to Blockchain Dreams: Empowering Women, One Pixel at a Time
By Amaranta Martínez "SUPERAMA"

As Superama, a muralist known for my vibrant and captivating works, I've always pushed the boundaries beyond the canvas. Walls, screens, clothes, shoes, any surface becomes a potential platform for my artistry. Fueled by an insatiable curiosity, I yearn to translate emotions and stories into living narratives. So, when Web3 emerged, it felt like a whole new canvas waiting to be splashed with vibrant possibility.

Web3, this decentralized and collaborative ecosystem, resonated deeply with my artistic spirit. It promised a future where the lines between creators and audiences blurred, fostering a collaborative spirit unlike anything I'd encountered. Yet, amidst the excitement, a stark reality remained: the voices of talented women were often underrepresented.

This ignited a new purpose in my artistic journey – to become a champion for the incredible women shaping the future of Web3.

But this journey wasn't a solo venture. I was fortunate enough to embark on this adventure alongside a phenomenal community of women who shared the same yearning for growth. We weren't just diving headfirst into this new technology and its opportunities; we were also learning new ways to create a space with more equity. It was a sisterhood of exploration, a supportive network where we could learn from each other's experiences and empower each other to push boundaries.

There were moments, of course, when doubt crept in. The whispers of skepticism, the dismissive glances from those who saw Web3 as a fad or worse, a scam. But in this community, judgment was replaced by unwavering support. We listened to each other's voices, even when they were shaky with uncertainty. We celebrated each other's victories, big and small. We lifted each other up, opening doors not just out of convenience, but because of the invisible thread that connected us, a thread woven from shared experience and a deep belief in the transformative power of Web3.

The beauty of Web3 unfolded before us – it wasn't just about geographical borders dissolving; it was about cultural barriers crumbling. Here, I found myself connecting with women from across the globe, women who spoke different languages, who came from vastly different backgrounds, and some who had never even dipped their toes into the world of art. Web3, in its essence, is a giant paintbrush, one that allows us to paint a future where these limitations are mere whispers of the past.

Truth be told, even with my insatiable curiosity, I wouldn't have continued this journey alone. Web3, for all its potential, could be a daunting space. The technical jargon, the constant evolution, the moments of doubt – these could easily chip away at even the most enthusiastic explorer. But the women I met, some who have become close friends, were the anchor that kept me grounded. Their unwavering support, their shared passion, and their belief in the power of our collective vision – that's what fueled my artistic journey in Web3.

This chapter explores the impact of this incredible community on my artistic journey. It delves into the experiences of fostering a supportive network for women in Web3, highlighting the challenges and triumphs encountered along the way. Through personal anecdotes and insights, I hope to inspire and empower others, particularly women, to join this movement towards a more equitable future. By co-creating a masterpiece of inclusivity on this ever-evolving canvas, Web3 holds the potential for every woman to find her voice and share her vibrant colors with the world.

Web3 Equity Community in Miami

The Power of Community

The catalyst for my Web3 adventure wasn't a technological trend, but rather the incredible women I surrounded myself with. A few years ago, I reconnected with Carla Curiel, a fellow entrepreneur and twin mom from the Dominican Republic. Carla, known for her passion for positive change and creating impactful content, introduced me to Web3 Equity, an organization she was involved in.

Web3 Equity resonated deeply with me – a global network of women from diverse backgrounds, united by a shared desire to learn, collaborate, and empower each other in the Web3 space. Their goal – creating an NFT collection celebrating female empowerment and fostering a more equitable space for women – perfectly aligned with my own artistic values.

NFT Collection I created for Web3 Equity

Taking the Leap: My First NFT Project

Through Carla's connection, I met Michelle Abbs, the founder of Web3 Equity. Our instant connection solidified the feeling that this was more than just a project; it was a movement I wholeheartedly wanted to be a part of. They offered me a fantastic opportunity – to create my first generative NFT collection, featuring the theme of "women who have a voice." This project allowed me to not only showcase my signature artistic style but also contribute to a cause I deeply believed in. The chance to collaborate with such inspiring women while being compensated for my work was truly fulfilling.

This experience at Web3 Equity served as a microcosm of the transformative power of Web3. Here, technology wasn't just about innovation; it was a tool for fostering inclusivity and empowering underrepresented voices. The project not only championed female artists but also showcased the potential of NFTs to create a more equitable space within the art world.

Fueled by the Web3 Equity experience, I poured my creative energy into my first NFT collection "Tuttle Tribe." This vibrant collection, bursting with the colors of Miami, paid homage to Julia Tuttle, the pioneering "Mother of Miami." But this collection wasn't just about a single woman; it was a celebration of diversity. I made sure that every type of woman was represented, reflecting the rich tapestry of Miami's multicultural soul.

The launch of Tuttle Tribe proved to be a phenomenal success. The supportive Web3 Equity community grew even stronger, with our monthly meetups becoming vibrant learning grounds. I even had the opportunity to share my knowledge, leading a session on how to integrate Artificial Intelligence (AI) and Augmented Reality (AR) into artwork. This exchange of knowledge and skills fostered a truly collaborative environment.

Miami itself embraced the project. The launch day was marked by a spectacular event at the prestigious Perez Art Museum, drawing over 400 attendees. Standing on that podium, addressing the enthusiastic crowd, I felt a surge of pride. It wasn't just about the artistic success of Tuttle Tribe. It was a testament to the power of women coming together to create positive change. This event highlighted the potential of Web3 to not only empower women artists but also bridge the gap between the traditional art world and the burgeoning realm of blockchain technology.

Speaking at the Perez Art Museum in Downtown Miami

Our community kept growing. We did an amazing side event in New York while NFT NYC was happening. My 2 years in Web3 Equity left me with so much knowledge, amazing relationships, and a boost of confidence that changed my life forever. We grew so much together and helped onboard so many amazing women in this ecosystem that was so new to all of us. After that, I had so much support and confidence, that I started to apply for many open calls, exhibitions, and speaker opportunities. Before entering this space, I would have never thought that my life as an artist was going to change forever.

Empowered by Women, Reaching the Moon

My journey into Web3 wasn't a solo flight; it was a collaborative adventure fueled by incredible women of the Web3 ecosystem. Surrounded by their passion and expertise, I embarked on a steep learning curve. These amazing women not only welcomed me with open arms but also opened doors to incredible opportunities. Through them, I connected with other inspiring communities like **World of Women**, leading to several impactful collaborative projects. These experiences, spanning over two years, equipped me with the confidence and skills to propel myself to unimaginable heights.

A Year of Transformation:

I'm excited to share with you some of the life-changing accomplishments I've been so grateful to experience in the past year. These incredible opportunities represent a turning point in my artistic journey. I'm still amazed by the remarkable things that unfolded!

My artwork was exhibited in Times Square and the Javits Convention Center in NYC

Speaker at NFT NYC 2024: I had the privilege of speaking at the prestigious NFT NYC conference, a major event bringing together the brightest minds in the Web3 space. Sharing my artistic journey and insights with such a receptive audience was incredibly rewarding.

Times Square Takeover: Imagine seeing your artwork displayed on a massive screen in the heart of Times Square! During the same week as NFT NYC, my work graced the iconic screens of Times Square, an incredible validation of my artistic evolution.

Miami Art Basel: I exhibited my work during Miami Art Basel, the pinnacle event of the city's artistic calendar. Being part of this vibrant scene, showcasing my art alongside established names, was a surreal and fulfilling experience.

Web3 Recognition: The incredible platform THE HUG, known for empowering artists of all backgrounds, featured me in an interview with Randi Zuckerberg, one of the co-founders. This recognition by such a respected organization further solidified my belief in the power of Web3 to connect and celebrate artists. That same week I exhibited my digital art at the CANVAS 3.0 a gallery inside the World Trade Center and at the HUG FEST it was announced that I was one of the 100 hundred artists to watch in 2024.

Interview with Randi Zuckerberg Co-Founder of THE HUG at the NYC exhibition inside the World Trade Center

Bitcoin Art History: Further etching my name in the Web3 landscape, I participated in a collection that Xverse & Gamma put together. This prestigious collection, showcasing the work of 10 Latin artists, was exhibited during the Bitcoin Conference in Nashville. It was also exhibited in Mexico for a Meet Up of Ordinals LATAM in Mexico City. This was my first collection on Bitcoin and it was sold out in 5 days!

My First Museum Exhibition: Exhibiting my digital artwork at the International Barroco Museum in Puebla, Mexico, during the Unlock Summit was an extraordinary experience. The museum dedicated an entire floor to projecting my art, creating an immersive environment where each piece came to life on a grand scale. The fusion of the museum architecture with my contemporary digital creations added a unique dimension to the display, making it a truly unforgettable moment in my artistic journey. The event was a celebration of innovation and creativity, and having my work featured in such a prestigious venue was an honor.

My work exhibited in an immersive exhibition at the Museo Internacional del Barroco in Puebla

Art on the Moon! The boundaries of artistic expression truly shattered the moment I received the news: my work, titled "Self Love," had been chosen for inclusion in the Lunaprise Museum – the first digital museum on the moon! In February 2024, a rocket roared skyward from Cape Canaveral, carrying a piece of my soul – a digital artwork that championed self-acceptance and reflection. This wasn't just any launch; it was my art, a vibrant exploration of self-worth, blasting off to become a permanent part of the lunar archive.

This incredible honor, shared with 21 other visionary artists, came as part of the Bitbasel CryptoArt for Impact Challenge, perfectly aligning with my own artistic mission. "Self Love" wasn't just a title; it was a message beamed towards the moon, a reminder to embrace ourselves with kindness and shatter the shackles of self-criticism. Witnessing my art become part of this historic lunar collection was a powerful moment, solidifying the transformative potential of art and its ability to transcend physical limitations.

Day of the rocket launch at Cape Canaveral where our artwork left the earth inside the Lunaprise Museum

This whole rush of amazing things happening, one after another, showed me just how powerful this incredible group of women I found really was. It wasn't just about making art anymore. It was about building this amazing network of support, like a band of sisters who broke down all the walls and pushed creativity to places we never thought possible. Looking back at the artist I used to be, this past year feels like something out of a movie. It shows what can happen when you take a chance and believe in yourself, especially when you have all this encouragement and new chances coming your way from these awesome women I met.

The truth is, jumping into Web3 wasn't all sunshine and rainbows. It took guts to explore this whole new way of making art. But you know what? Taking that risk, that's what led me to all these incredible experiences. It's like stepping off a ledge, trusting you'll fly. And guess what? I flew to the moon!

My Women of Web3

Being part of Women of Web3 as their Digital Arts Director has been nothing short of life changing. It's a community that thrives on empowerment, innovation, and collaboration, giving women like me the tools and connections to thrive in a rapidly evolving ecosystem. The support I've found here has been a constant source of inspiration, fueling my passion and confidence to embrace challenges and seize opportunities I never thought possible. This journey has reminded me of the power of unity, proving that when women come together, the possibilities are limitless.

Joining Women of Web3 has been a transformative journey, opening doors I never imagined possible. Through this vibrant and supportive community, I've built meaningful connections that have propelled my career to new heights. One of the most remarkable moments was speaking at the United Nations during the 79th Science Summit, where I shared my journey as an artist navigating the Web3 ecosystem. Women of Web3's unwavering support has been instrumental in creating opportunities not just for me but for countless Latina women.

I can't wait to see what the future holds for Women of Web3 — a community that has already accomplished so much and continues to inspire limitless possibilities. Being part of this creative, empowering team is an honor that fills me with pride and gratitude. Together, we are shaping a future where women lead with innovation, courage, and boundless creativity. This is only the beginning, and I know that the impact we're making today will ripple through generations to come. The journey ahead is bright, and I'm so thrilled to be walking it hand in hand with such extraordinary women.

Conclusion

This journey, a whirlwind of artistic growth fueled by a passion to champion women in this exciting new creative space, feels like a love letter to the amazing women I met. These incredible artists, each a shining star in their own right, shared my vision and lit a fire in my soul. Together, we built a welcoming space for everyone, a place where dreams could take flight, fueled by our shared goals and the power of believing in each other. We opened doors that once seemed impossible, leading to incredible opportunities that dazzled even the wildest dreams I used to have.

What started as a solo adventure to explore my art became a powerful example of what happens when women support each other. We joined forces, like a wave crashing down on barriers, and achieved incredible things. From speaking at big conferences to having my art displayed in amazing places, and even blasting off to the moon, these accomplishments showcase what's possible when women dare to dream big.

This story is a call to action, an invitation for all the amazing innovators, particularly women out there to share their unique voices and talents. Let's create a future that's full of life and color, a masterpiece built on teamwork and the joy of seeing each other succeed. Dream without limits, because there's room for everyone on this ever-changing canvas, and a light waiting for every woman to claim.

Let's Connect

Amaranta Martínez
www.womenofweb3un.io/speakers/amaranta-martinez

AFTERWORD

Dani Mariano, President of Razorfish and a champion for women in technology

In the burgeoning world of Web3, a revolution is quietly unfolding. With women representing just 7% of Web3 founders and 27% of employees across crypto startups, being a female in this space means being an activist (Accenture, 2020). Women in the Web3 Space – Inclusive Futures is a capsule from the frontlines of this revolution. These are stories of resilience, creativity, and personal transformation with powerful messages about how to build a more equitable future for all.

This collection inspired me in so many ways, from overcoming adversity and innovating relentlessly to being a mentor and fostering community. These stories are crucial to document and celebrate. From artists and muralists to chief operating officers and developers, each uniquely contributes to a tapestry of women helping women with courage, creativity, and collaboration woven throughout.

No matter where you come from, Web3 creates unparalleled opportunities for women and marginalized communities. From small villages and the bustling streets of New York to the serene landscapes of the Moon, these stories can teach us all about what is possible when we combine the fibers of imagination with the transformative power of technology.

Adversity Fuels Resiliency

While others may allow a myriad of challenges to stifle their ambitions, these women choose to relentlessly pursue their dreams in the face of adversity. Débora Betsabé Carrizo's story is emblematic of the spirit that pervades this collection. Growing up in Mendoza, Argentina, she saw education as her path to a better future, later crossing borders and cultures to fulfill her dreams. She used the challenge of being the only woman in male-dominated technology labs as fuel to be the best.

Carley Beck shared how her story would be, "one of hope and beauty, focusing on positivity and resilience." She advises us all to redefine ourselves as more than our painful traumas and our greatest accomplishments, reminding us "you are enough."

Empowerment Through Technology

This collection also exemplifies the transformative power of Web3 technology—not just as a tool for financial innovation, but as a platform for empowerment. As Leslie Motta wrote, "Web3 was not just a professional pivot, but a personal awakening—a realization that this technology had the power to transform lives, including my own."

From creating decentralized applications that offer unprecedented access to resources, to leveraging blockchain for greater transparency and security, these women are at the forefront of technological empowerment. Their projects do not settle for innovation alone. They set out to inspire others, and in doing so, create an undeniable momentum within the Web3 community.

Wildy Martinez's first NFT sale launched her transformation. "I felt so empowered for the first time in a long time. Web3 represented a shift towards a more user-centric internet, where individuals have greater control and ownership over their digital lives, and where transparency and trust are enhanced through decentralized technologies." Martinez aptly describes the way many of us have experienced the emerging tech space as a great force for democratization and co-creation.

Community as a Verb

Many of these stories demonstrate a shared redefinition of community. Instead of a group of people, community becomes an action. Starting mentorship and education programs, collaborative projects, and community-driven initiatives, these women have forged networks of support that extend well beyond the digital realm to actively lift each other up.

Marisa Estrada Rivera's mission is one such example. She represents marginalized communities in her work as a member of the National Policy Network of Women of Color in Blockchain by advocating for inclusive policies on Capitol Hill. She is also the curator and organizer of Hola Metaverso to create a welcoming space for women to enter the Web3 space on two continents.

Giving Back: A Cycle of Generosity

Giving back is another recurring theme, illustrated by initiatives like that of Leslie Motta. Her Women of Basketball NFT project supports junior college female athletes. Beyond providing scholarships, the project brings attention to the challenges young women athletes face through action.

Ana Isabel Rivas and Mauricio Cruz commemorated the historic Web3 session at UNGA78 with the "Guiding Light" NFT. It represents the 17 women who brought their voice to the global stage, with 100% of the profits going towards scholarships for Science, Technology, Engineering, and Mathematics courses for girls and teenagers. These efforts underscore a profound commitment to using Web3 not just for personal or professional gain but to contribute to societal good.

These are just two examples where women in this book create a cycle of generosity that propels the community forward, ensuring that the benefits of Web3 technology reach all corners of society.

Inclusion: The Heart of Web3

Inclusion is the ethos of Web3. As advisors to the Women of Web3, Mauricio Cruz and Amaranta Martinez understand the value of diversity. Mauricio is dedicated to mentoring women, championing women's projects, and creating endless opportunities for women to thrive in the Web3 space. Amaranta's work with Web3 Equity and her first generative NFT collection "Turtle Tribe" celebrating every type of woman, stands as a powerful symbol of diversity and inclusion.

Sandy Martinez shared how, with Cyndi Coon, she achieved her dream of speaking at the United Nations with the UNGA78 session, "Women in the Web3 Space: Reducing Inequalities Through Digital and Technological Opportunities." This history making session was the first all-women Web3 and blockchain panel at the UN, with 70% Latina representation and highlighted the importance and power of diverse voices shaping the future of Web3.

These chapters describe the way these leaders create spaces where everyone can thrive, regardless of background or identity, making their impact truly revolutionary.

A Call to Action: Building an equitable future for all

As we look to the future, the case for diversity is clear. Diverse teams understand diverse customers and accelerate innovation. They also drive outsized performance. According to McKinsey's report "Diversity Matters More", top-quartile diverse companies had a 39% greater likelihood of outperforming competitors with diverse teams (2023).

More urgently, the technology innovation cycle is accelerating. Bias, found throughout the data sets training the current artificial intelligence cycle, is the enemy of a more equitable global future. Diverse perspectives combined with the blockchain's capability to record provenance with transparency play a critical role in ensuring the representation of marginalized communities.

As you have read throughout this collection, there are many ways to contribute to this mission and co-create an equitable future. Bringing together their wisdom in an actionable list, here are some ways we can each drive change.

1. **Show Up.** Attend Web3 events, organize your own gatherings, speak on panels and join digital events. Often, showing up is just the beginning. No matter where you're starting from, you will have an important role in developing the Web3 ecosystem and bringing women along with us.
2. **Be a Mentor.** We are at the beginning of the Web3 era. Mentoring just one other person will help shape the future of this industry through your knowledge and experience, fostering a culture of learning and growth.
3. **Amplify Voices.** Use your platform to highlight the work of others, ensuring the contributions of other women are recognized and celebrated.
4. **Collaborate and Connect.** Engage in projects that prioritize diversity and inclusivity, creating opportunities for women to lead and innovate. Spend time building networks and meeting new people. Create win-win momentum through collaboration.
5. **Invest.** Support women-led initiatives and startups in Web3, providing the financial backing necessary for their ideas to flourish. That first taste of success will instill confidence and spark determination for others just starting out.
6. **Insist on Inclusion.** Demand diversity and don't settle for less. No matter what seat you have at the table, holding a standard for inclusion will promote gender equality and empower women to succeed.

As I reflect on the journeys of each author and their serendipitous encounters with Web3, I'm reminded of my own entry into digital marketing and eventually the Web3 world. The idea of connecting marketing to people through technology was thrilling because, as Débora Betsabé Carrizo wrote, "when we are inside the technology field, we are creators." I am grateful to the friends and colleagues who told me I was crazy as much as I am for the mentors who helped me find my way.

These stories will inspire new generations of women to overcome challenges, use their voice in the male dominated rooms, and achieve what has never been done before. With courage and passion, let's converge on the frontier of Web3 that promises a future as boundless as our aspirations.

To Ana Isabel, Carley, Débora, Leslie, Ritzy, Sandy and Wildy: Thank you for dreaming big. Thank you for reaching your hand back to bring other women with you. And thank you for leading the change we want to see in the world.

GLOSSARY

This glossary provides a foundation for understanding the key terms and concepts that will guide readers as they explore the world of Web3 through the stories and experiences shared in this book

Get Started Basics Terminology

Alpha: A slang term for "intelligence." Those who own alpha have information that the rest of the market does not yet know. These people spend hours upon hours finding undiscovered projects and sometimes sharing them on Twitter or other social media. Usually in reference to NFT projects but can also apply to cryptocurrency.

Blockchain: A distributed database or ledger that is shared between nodes in a computer network. Like a database, a blockchain stores information electronically in a digital format. Blockchains are best known for their crucial role in cryptocurrency systems, such as Bitcoin, in maintaining a secure and decentralized record of transactions. The innovation with blockchain is that it guarantees the fidelity and security of a data record and generates trust without the need for a trusted third party.

Crypto Currency: Cryptocurrency, also called virtual currency or cryptocurrency, is digital money. That means no physical coins or bills—it's all online. It uses cryptographic methods to secure your financial transactions, control the creation of new units, and verify the transfer of assets. Therefore, we can consider them a decentralized alternative to digital currencies. With the term "decentralized," we mean that these currencies are not controlled by a single service, company, or bank. The first cryptocurrency was Bitcoin in 2009. The most recognized are Bitcoin, Ethereum, Tether, Binance Coin, USD Coin, XRP, Terra, Solana, Cardano, and Avalanche.

DAO (Decentralized Autonomous Organization): An organization represented by rules encoded as a computer program, controlled by organization members, and not by a central authority. DAOs make decisions through a consensus mechanism, often using tokens for voting.

Floor Price: The floor or floor price is the lowest price to buy an NFT in the secondary market. It is the most popular metric for tracking the performance of an NFT collection over time and comparing it to others.

Metaverse: A collective virtual shared space, created by the convergence of virtually enhanced physical reality and physically persistent virtual spaces. In Web3, it's often a fully immersive, 3D digital environment where users can interact socially and economically as a digital figure, work, and play.

Minting: The process of validating information, such as domain ownership, and recording it on the blockchain. The beauty of any NFT minting is that all transactions can be viewed in the ledger, so anyone can verify that they were successfully minted. In most collections, this is an important moment.

NFT (Non-Fungible Token): A unique digital asset representing ownership or proof of authenticity of a specific item, typically digital art, music, videos, or in-game items, stored on a blockchain. NFT assets can be bought and sold online with digital currencies like any other property with the verification and validation of the transaction made on the blockchain. NFTs are assigned a kind of digital certificate of authenticity, a series of metadata that cannot be modified.

PFP (Acronym for "profile image."): NFT holders or investors often use their PFP of their favorite project to symbolize they are part of that community or as their personal brand.

Real-World Assets (RWAs): Real-World Assets (RWAs) refer to tangible or physical assets, such as real estate, commodities, art, and other forms of traditional investments, that are tokenized and represented on the blockchain. By digitizing these assets, RWAs enable broader access, liquidity, and fractional ownership in decentralized finance (DeFi) ecosystems, allowing more people to invest in traditionally exclusive markets. Tokenization of RWAs bridges the gap between traditional finance and blockchain technology, creating new opportunities for asset management and financial inclusion.

Rugged: A term used to describe being scammed or cheated by the creators of a Web3 project.

Smart Contract: Self-executing contracts with the terms of the agreement directly written into code. They automatically enforce and execute agreements based on pre-set conditions, without needing intermediaries.

Token: A digital unit of value issued on a blockchain, representing an asset, utility, or voting rights within a specific ecosystem. Tokens can be fungible (like cryptocurrencies) or non-fungible (like NFTs).

Web3: The next generation of the internet, focusing on decentralized platforms and services, where users have greater control over their data and interactions, often leveraging blockchain technology.

Whitelist: Whitelists are highly coveted, and fans will do almost anything to earn one. The race to "WL" sees people dig up insider information on a project before it's released, join the project's Discord as "OG," and enter giveaways via Twitter. Think of it like a "VIP" list to enter into a project.

Software & Applications

Blockchain Explorer: A tool that allows users to search and view details about blockchain transactions, blocks, addresses, and other data in real-time. Examples include Etherscan for Ethereum or Blockchain.info for Bitcoin.

Consensus Mechanism: The method used by blockchain networks to agree on the state of the ledger. Common types include Proof of Work (PoW) and Proof of Stake (PoS).

DApp (Decentralized Application): An application built on a decentralized network that combines a smart contract with a frontend user interface. Unlike traditional apps, DApps run on blockchain technology, giving users more control and transparency.

DeFi (Decentralized Finance): A movement that leverages blockchain technology to recreate traditional financial systems—like lending, borrowing, and trading—in a decentralized, open, and permissionless manner.

Digital Wallet: A software application (hot) or hardware device (cold) that is used to store the private keys of the blockchain assets: your cryptocurrency and NFTs. Wallets are used to verify token ownership, mint listing status, and more. This is usually the number one job for anyone starting their Web3 journey. An example of a digital wallet is MetaMask.

Discord: Discord's servers are organized into topic-based channels where you can collaborate, share, and just talk about your day without clogging up a group chat. This platform is used for official communication for various NFT projects. There are different channels like general chats, chats in different languages, voice channels, and announcements. It has video chat capabilities too.

Gas Fees: The fees required to conduct transactions on a blockchain, typically paid to miners or validators who process and confirm transactions. Gas fees can vary depending on network congestion.

Hardware Ledger (often referred to as a hardware wallet): This is one of the most secure ways to protect your digital assets. These devices store your private keys offline, away from the reach of hackers and malware, significantly reducing the risk of theft. By keeping your digital assets secure with a hardware ledger, you ensure that your investments remain under your control and safe from potential cyber threats.

IPFS (InterPlanetary File System): A peer-to-peer file-sharing system designed to make the web faster, safer, and more open. IPFS allows users to store and share files in a decentralized manner.

Layer 2 Solutions: Technologies or protocols built on top of a blockchain (Layer 1) to improve scalability and transaction speed. Examples include the Lightning Network for Bitcoin and Optimism for Ethereum.

Tokenomics: The study of the economic system within a blockchain project, including the creation, distribution, and incentive structures of tokens within the ecosystem.

Twitter or X Spaces: A platform where live audio social conversations happen on Twitter's social platform. They are like interactive podcasts. Spaces are public, and you can join one of three ways. Each space has a public link or a link that a host or listener can include in a Tweet or share via direct message. Live Spaces with a speaker or presenter you follow will also appear at the top of your timeline or home page, highlighted in purple.

OUR PARTNERS IN IMPACT

FEATURED SPEAKERS

Women of Web3 is honored to feature the voices of extraordinary women from around the world that adding value to the digital landscape and the global conversation on diversity, inclusion, and innovation, sharing insights at the Women of Web3 United Nations sessions and beyond. We are immensely proud to witness each of these incredible women uplifting and empowering each other, speaking each other's names in rooms of opportunity. This is how true impact is made. Together, we are not just building a movement; we are creating lasting change.

Science Summit at UNGA78
12-29 September 2023

Science Summit at UNGA79
10 - 27 September 2024

Ana Isabel Rivas Fernandez – Mexico
Carley Beck – Canada
Cyndi Coon – United States
Débora Carrizo – Argentina
Elizabeth Leon González – Puerto Rico
Gianina Skarlett – Venezuela
Leslie Motta – Mexico
Lizeth Jaramillo – Colombia
Lucia Diaz – Colombia
Marisa Estrada – Mexico
Maryam Taguri – Canada
Michelle Bird – Puerto Rico
Sandra Martinez – Mexico
Sandy Carter – United States
Selena Scott – United States
Sofia Vera Reyes – Mexico
Wildy Martinez – Dominican Republic

Liseli Akayombokwa – Zambia
Tove Andersson – Sweden
Shreya Bhan – India
Shana Douglas – United States
Diana Cañas – Colombia
Melina Giubilaro – Canada
Lucia Iturriaga – Mexico
Mulenga Kapwepwe – Zambia
Wendy Lopez – Colombia & Mexico
Dani Mariano – United States
Amaranta Martinez – Venezuela
Rainbow Mosho – Greece & United States
Jenifer Pepen – Dominican Republic
Ambriel Pouncy – United States
Sol Falco "Sol Siete" – Argentina

Special Guest:
Carrie Lyn Henman – United States

CLAIM BLOSSOM AWAKENING NFT

Blossom Awakening

"Blossom Awakening" is a captivating AI-generated digital collectible, enhanced by an augmented reality (AR) feature that brings the piece to life. The artwork portrays a powerful woman surrounded by vibrant flowers, symbolizing empowerment, resilience, and growth. As AR butterflies emerge from the flowers, the dynamic composition reflects the transformative nature of women who lead, innovate, and evolve.

This collectible aligns with the United Nations Sustainable Development Goals 5 and 10, championing gender equality and sustainability. With its immersive AR experience, *Blossom Awakening* represents women blooming in their own space, setting an example for future generations through strength and leadership.

Artist Info

Wildy Martinez, the visionary behind Wildflower Fields, and **Amaranta Martinez**, known as SUPERAMA, unite their creative forces in *Blossom Awakening*. Wildy, an internationally recognized fashion designer and artist, pioneers the use of Web3 and AI technologies in her work, advocating for representation and proudly supporting the vitiligo community. Amaranta, a highly acclaimed visual artist from Venezuela based in Miami, has received numerous prestigious awards, including an Emmy Award, for her impactful and emotionally resonant creations. Together, they blend their expertise in fashion, technology, and social advocacy, creating art that champions women's empowerment and celebrates diversity.

CLAIM YOUR WOMEN OF WEB3 NFT

SCAN THE QR CODE OR VISIT THE LINK BELOW TO CLAIM YOUR EXCLUSIVE DIGITAL COLLECTIBLE

WWW.THEGALLERIA.APP/DROP/ WW3-BLOSSOM-AWAKENING

BRING THIS ART TO LIFE WITH YOUR SMARTPHONE

1. INSTALL THE ARTIVIVE APP ON YOUR SMARTPHONE
2. SCAN THE ARTWORK ABOVE WITH THE APP TO VIEW THE AR FEATURE
4. RECORD, SHARE & TAG US!

Copyright Turkey Hill Press ©2024

Made in the USA
Monee, IL
01 December 2024

71893929R00118